THE RIGHT CLIMATE FOR CARBON TAXES:
Creating Economic Incentives to Protect the Atmosphere

Roger C. Dower (WRI)
and
Mary Beth Zimmerman
(Alliance to Save Energy)

WORLD RESOURCES INSTITUTE

August 1992

Kathleen Courrier
Publications Director

Brooks Clapp
Marketing Manager

Hyacinth Billings
Production Manager

Ecomedia; James MacKenzie
Cover Photos

Each World Resources Institute Report represents a timely, scholarly treatment of a subject of public concern. WRI takes responsibility for choosing the study topics and guaranteeing its authors and researchers freedom of inquiry. It also solicits and responds to the guidance of advisory panels and expert reviewers. Unless otherwise stated, however, all the interpretation and findings set forth in WRI publications are those of the authors.

CONTENTS

ACKNOWLEDGMENTS

We wish to thank those who helped us with the research and production of this report. In particular, we want to acknowledge the careful research assistance of Fiona Mullins and Sean Fox. The report has benefited greatly from generous and thoughtful comments of many colleagues. From within WRI we thank Alan Brewster, Keith Kozloff, Jessica Mathews, Jim MacKenzie, Rafe Pomerance, Walt Reid, and Robert Repetto. We also express our gratitude to outside reviewers who include Marc Chupka, Andrew Dean, Dawn Erlandson, Dale Jorgensen, Daniel Lashof, Alan Miller, Richard D. Morgenstern, Matthias Mors, Richard L. Ottinger, Paul Portney, Max Sawicky, and Bob Shackleton. Ultimately, of course, the authors alone are responsible for the accuracy and recommendations of the report.

Our special thanks to Kathleen Courrier for her skillful editing of the report, to Robbie Nichols for her editing and writing assistance, to Hyacinth Billings for her management of the production process, to Allyn Massey for preparing the figures, to Sue Terry for her help in obtaining numerous reports and references, to our Policy Affairs Program for the oversight and management of the distribution process, to Kevin Parker for participating in the development of the project, to Cindy Barger for her assistance and coordination at every stage, and Eva Vasiliades for her day-to-day support of the project.

Finally, our gratitude to WRI President Gus Speth for his overall guidance and continual support.

R.C.D.
M.B.Z.

FOREWORD

Taxing carbon dioxide emissions may be an idea whose time is at hand in the United States, now that reducing greenhouse gas emissions has become an international imperative. Such consequences of fossil fuel use as smog and acid rain—and their impacts on forests, crops, lakes, and the air we breathe—have been evident for many years. But the argument for carbon taxes is a relatively new one: that they represent the most promising solution to one of society's biggest problems, accelerated climate change.

Some 150 nations, including the United States, signed the climate treaty that was the centerpiece of the Rio Earth Summit, agreeing to begin taking steps aimed at controlling greenhouse gas emissions. Carbon dioxide—the leading greenhouse gas and an inevitable by-product of fossil fuel burning—is a prime target for reductions if the greenhouse threat is to be defused.

Make no mistake about it, the threat is real. For scientists, the question is no longer *whether* the earth will heat up, but how much it will heat up, and how soon. The latest estimate by the Intergovernmental Panel on Climate Change is that the global average temperature will rise by from 1.5 to 3 degrees Centigrade over 1900 levels by the middle of the next century. That may not sound like much, but a few degrees can spell enormous change: during the depths of the last ice age, for instance, the earth was only 5 degrees Centigrade colder than it is now. Temperatures at the midlatitudes are expected to rise about twice as much as the global average temperature does. Together with declining rainfall, this could bring dust-bowl conditions to the American Great Plains and some Eurasian farmlands. The expected 48-centimeter rise in sea levels would devastate low-lying coasts and islands, especially if tropical storms become more fearsome in a climate-altered world. All these changes may outpace the ability of species to move to new habitats or adapt to changing conditions, exacerbating the species extinction crisis already in progress.

In *The Right Climate for Carbon Taxes: Creating Economic Incentives to Protect the Atmosphere,*

Roger C. Dower, director of WRI's program on climate, energy, and pollution, and Mary Beth Zimmerman, program manager at the Alliance to Save Energy, make a compelling case for using carbon taxes to meet the goals implied by the climate treaty. They maintain that carbon taxes are the least costly way to encourage carbon dioxide reductions from the economy. By forcing energy prices to reflect the risks of climate change, carbon taxes would create economic incentives to use less-carbon-intensive fuels and products. Properly set, carbon taxes would encourage the cheapest reductions first and ensure that reductions are achieved as cost-effectively as possible. Compared to alternative approaches, carbon taxes are comprehensive and flexible, allowing the market to chose where and how reductions will occur. Moreover, carbon taxes would spur technological innovations in the way energy is used and supplied.

Mr. Dower and Ms. Zimmerman argue that carbon taxes would benefit the U.S. economy as a whole if adopted as part of an overall shift of the tax burden toward things we want to discourage, such as pollution, and away from things we want to encourage, such as work and savings. Carbon taxes would mean that some energy prices would rise, but the authors detail ways to cushion the added expense. For businesses, higher energy prices could be partly offset, for example, by higher investment tax credits. A higher earned-income tax credit could help balance things out for low-income working families. Equity for regional dislocations could be built in by earmarking part of the carbon tax revenues for state grants to provide retraining programs for dislocated workers. Phasing in such a tax over a period of years would give producers and consumers time to adapt to higher prices.

The Right Climate for Carbon Taxes is the latest in the World Resources Institute's continuing series of reports on climate, energy, and pollution policies. This report's recommendations extend those of such previous WRI studies as *The Going Rate: What it Really Costs to Drive; Driving Forces: Motor Vehicle Trends and their Implications for Global Warming,*

Energy Strategies, and Transportation Planning; Breathing Easier: Taking Action on Climate Change, Air Pollution, and Energy Insecurity; and *Energy for a Sustainable World.*

We would like to thank Alida Rockefeller for her support of our research on carbon taxes. We are also grateful for the support the following foundations have provided for this work and for other research projects on climate, energy, and pollution: Public Welfare Foundation, Inc.; Rockefeller Brothers Fund; W. Alton Jones Foundation, Inc.; The Joyce Founda-tion; Charles Stewart Mott Foundation; The George Gund Foundation; The William Penn Foundation; The Energy Foundation; The Joyce Mertz-Gilmore Foundation; and the German Marshall Fund of the United States. To all of these, we express our deep appreciation.

James Gustave Speth
President
World Resources Institute

I. INTRODUCTION

International concern over the potential for carbon dioxide and other "greenhouse gas" emissions to change the world's climate has generated national and international debate over the most appropriate policy responses for reducing these emissions. In particular, countries are searching for emission-reduction tools that are cost-effective, consistent with continued economic growth, and equitable with respect to both costs and benefits.

Any number of studies have shown that a pollution tax on carbon dioxide, a "carbon tax," is the most cost-effective means of reducing carbon dioxide emissions, the major greenhouse gas.[1] But the United States and many other countries have resisted pollution taxes in general, and carbon taxes in particular, as environmental policy tools. Much of this reticence stems from the alleged impacts of a tax-based pollution control strategy—in the case of a carbon tax, slower national economic growth, reduced international competitiveness, and a disproportionate burden on certain income groups and regions.

In fact, virtually all of the basic approaches to controlling CO_2 emissions entail economic costs and make some people or regions better off than others. Certainly, any effective CO_2-reduction program will raise the price of goods and services produced from carbon-based fuels. Like carbon taxes, regulatory strategies (often called "command and control" policies), and pollution permits for carbon emissions can reduce economic output and generate regional and income disparities.[2] These effects may be harder to trace in a regulation or permit system than in the case of carbon taxes, but they are no less real.

Compared to alternative approaches, however, carbon taxes have several clear economic benefits. In particular:

■ Carbon taxes offer a practical and administratively manageable means of encouraging a "least cost" approach to achieving any given level of reduction in carbon dioxide emissions. Compared to regulatory alternatives, they could save significant economic resources.

■ A portion of the revenues generated by a carbon tax can be returned to the economy by lowering other taxes, providing net gains for the U.S. economy; and

■ Some of the revenues from a carbon tax can also be used to compensate groups adversely affected by the tax.

Of course, dollars diverted to compensation programs may not be available to finance tax reform initiatives, and desires for economic efficiency must be balanced against those for fairness or equity. In the end, how tax revenues are allocated between the competing goals is a political call. Nevertheless, researchers can and should narrow the range of choices. Current economic modelling work helps policy-makers grasp the economic implications of recycling a large part of the revenues from a carbon tax and leaving the rest for other programs. In the future, a better understanding of how various allocations would affect various states could help build a firmer policy foundation and make it easier to determine the size and allocation formula for a block-grant scheme.

All the economic merits of a pollution or carbon tax notwithstanding, political barriers impede their implementation. The public is leery of new taxes. But pollsters' findings that the American public is willing to pay more for environmental protection imply that a pollution tax might be more politically acceptable than other types of taxes. A pollution tax that offsets other taxes would presumably be even more tolerable.

The biggest hurdle to more sensible tax policy is an underlying distrust of the system. The public does not believe that the government will raise one set of taxes only to lower another. Instead, it expects that any increase will result in more net spending. Any pollution tax strategy must be accompanied by policy initiatives for addressing this suspicion.

II. WHY TAX CARBON?

The combustion of fossil fuels to power homes, factories, businesses, cars, and trucks results in the discharge of a wide array of pollutants into our environment. While several of the pollutants from the burning of fossil fuels—among them, sulfur dioxide (SO_2), volatile organic compounds, particulates, and nitrogen oxides (NO_x)—are regulated by federal, state, and local governments, one major pollutant, carbon dioxide (CO_2), remains unconstrained. Man-made emissions of carbon dioxide are the leading cause of the build-up of greenhouse gas emissions, which trap heat and intensify the natural greenhouse effect, and may warm Earth's atmosphere. (In the United States, most of the carbon dioxide, some 1.5 billion U.S. tons of carbon per year, is released when fossil fuels are burned.)

The carbon contained in carbon dioxide emissions is not a conventional pollutant. It is not associated with immediate effects on health and the environment, and the full environmental impacts of CO_2 emissions take decades to unfold. But while scientists continue to debate the timing and degree of risk posed by global warming, consensus is solidifying on the likelihood of average global temperatures increasing as atmospheric concentrations of greenhouse gases rise.

The potential environmental and health impacts of rapidly rising global temperatures are the subject of significant current research and discussion. But what is already clear is that the environmental risks are potentially large and diverse. The local physical effects of increasing temperatures might include coastal erosion due to sea level rise or drought due to changing weather patterns. The ecological effects may include the loss of wetlands and numerous species or, if their ability to adapt fails to keep pace with rapidly moving climate zones, even entire ecosystems.[3] On the other hand, moderate levels of warming may entail some beneficial environmental impacts. No boons should be anticipated, but, for example, crop yields for certain plant varieties might increase as a result of increased CO_2 fertilization.

All of these changes ultimately have economic and political ramifications as well. Even if, for example, efforts are made to adapt to changing climate by building coastal defenses, the costs associated with the loss of agricultural and fisheries harvest, coastal-based tourism, and other economic activities, as well as the need for new water supply and drainage systems and so on, may well remain. Then too, many of the world's poorest people live on coastal or marginally productive lands and could be forced to migrate, perhaps triggering economic and political instabilities.

Without policy intervention, carbon dioxide emissions are expected to grow both in the United States and worldwide due to population growth, economic growth, and increased reliance on coal.

Without policy intervention, carbon dioxide emissions are expected to grow both in the United States and worldwide due to population growth, economic growth, and increased reliance on coal.[4] This result is common to many long-term energy forecasts or projections. For example, the National Energy Strategy estimates that, in the absence of policy changes, energy use in the United States will increase by 64 percent by 2030. Coal, which now accounts for 22 percent of total energy use will increase to 38 percent of total energy use in 2030. This trend is even more pronounced for other regions of the world. Scientists warn that avoiding unprecedented rates of climate change requires a reversal of this upward trend. The 1988 Toronto Conference suggested reducing carbon dioxide emissions by roughly 20 percent from current levels within a decade and making larger reductions thereafter.[5]

WHAT IS A CARBON TAX?

Any serious effort to reduce atmospheric concentrations of greenhouse gases will involve reducing CO_2 emissions.[6] This is not a simple problem. Carbon dioxide is emitted from millions of individual sources, ranging from cars and trucks to huge electric utilities. For each source, there are likely to be several alternatives for reducing CO_2 emissions. Fossil-fuel use is affected by consumer choices about how much heat, light, and other energy services they want to consume, how efficient their appliances are, and which type of energy their appliances use. Consumers also choose which non-energy goods and services they want to buy, and since some of these goods require more energy than others to make, they indirectly influence how much energy is used in manufacturing. For their part, manufacturers can typically choose whether to use relatively more labor and capital or relatively more energy in production, and they too can choose among energy types. Electric utilities can choose which fuels to use in generating power and, in many states, can also choose to buy or subsidize energy-efficient products for their consumers rather than to generate more power. Still another variable is whether consumers, manufactures, and utilities will replace their energy-using equipment if energy prices change or wait until they have to buy new equipment anyway. Cars can be driven less, driven more efficiently, or designed more efficiently. Industries that emit CO_2 can use less coal and more natural gas, invest in energy efficiency programs, change their mix of products, or do all three. Each of these options and opportunities is likely to have different costs. From an economic perspective, the public policy problem, simply stated, is how to induce responses like that at the lowest cost possible.

There are three basic approaches available to governments to encourage CO_2 reductions. Under the traditional approach to pollution control, emissions levels for each source would be set administratively, as would the means and strategies for achieving specified reductions. Such "command and control" or regulatory programs dictate the range of choices and decisions concerning carbon reductions that producers and consumers can make. To cost-effectively prompt CO_2 reductions, administrative

agencies would have to identify each source of CO_2 emissions, identify the least expensive way for each source to limit their emissions, and then monitor how well each source meets the requirements. For example, a regulatory control program for CO_2 might set automobile-efficiency standards, energy-efficiency standards for appliances, fuel-use requirements for electric utilities, and so on. Under this system, there is little incentive for any particular source to seek alternative, perhaps less expensive, ways of controlling their emissions of CO_2 once the requirements have been stipulated. Their performance is judged by their ability to meet the standards set by the administrative agency. The informational needs of a command-and-control approach to CO_2 reductions are huge and the analytical prerequisites—that is, knowing in advance the least costly way for each source to reduce its emissions—are substantial.

Under a 'command and control' system, there is little incentive for any particular source to seek alternative, perhaps less expensive, ways of controlling their emissions of CO_2 once the requirements have been stipulated.

The other two approaches to controlling carbon dioxide emissions rely more on economic incentives to encourage reductions and less on administrative requirements. Of these, one would be to impose a tax on the carbon content of fossil fuels. *(See Box 1.)* This approach to lowering CO_2 emissions can offer notable advantages over the traditional regulatory approach to pollution control.[7] By increasing the price of fossil fuels to reflect their contribution to the risks of climate change, carbon taxes create an economic incentive for each source of CO_2 to seek out reduction alternatives. In particular, once an overall level of desired emission reductions is set and the tax required to achieve those reductions is in place, governments need not set an emission level and control option for each and every source of CO_2. With a carbon tax, many of the administrative costs of trying to set the rules and standards for compliance are avoided, and a structure that minimizes the cost to the economy as a whole of achieving a CO_2 target is created.

The mechanics of a carbon tax are rather straightforward. As typically defined, the tax is levied on different fuels according to their carbon content, which is equivalent, in general, to their potential for emitting carbon dioxide when burned. A carbon tax would fall more heavily on coal than oil, which in turn would be taxed more than natural gas. To be most effective, the tax would be applied at the point that the fuel enters the economy—at the wellhead for natural gas, the minemouth for coal, and the well or dockside for oil. Under this scheme, taxing carbon early in the production chain allows policy-makers

to influence all decisions concerning fossil fuel use.[8]

The third basic tactic for CO_2 reductions involves the use of marketable CO_2 emission permits. Essentially, a marketable permit system would set the quantity of CO_2 emissions that could be released in any given year. Permits for this amount would be allocated to producers and consumers. They, in turn, would be free to buy and sell the permits among themselves. Unlike a carbon tax, a marketable permits system sets the quantity of emissions—not their price. The net economic effect can be similar, however. Utilities and other companies that can reduce their CO_2 emissions cheaply would find it in their economic interest to do so, rather than pay for emission permits. Alternatively, CO_2 emitters facing high

---

BOX 1: DEFINING A CARBON TAX

As defined here, a carbon tax is an excise tax on the producers of raw fossil fuels (sometimes called primary energy) based on the relative carbon content of the fuels. It is not a true emissions tax insofar as it is not pegged to the actual level of CO_2 emitted from a given source. Carbon taxes are, however, proportional to CO_2 emissions when fuel is burned if no cost-effective method of reducing CO_2 emissions

Table 1. Carbon Content of Selected Fossil Fuels (lbs of Carbon)

	By Volume	By Energy Content (Btu)*
Coal	1440.00 (ton)	2.04
Crude Oil	6.18 (gallon)	1.60
Natural Gas	0.03 (1000 ft³)	1.20
Gasoline	5.10 (gallon)	1.50

* (units are represented as 10^{-4} lbs per Btu)

from these gases is available. *(See Table 1.)* (Coal is the most carbon-intensive fuel per unit of heat released, followed by crude oil and then natural gas.)

Carbon taxes would appear to consumers and manufacturers as energy price increases. But since taxes would be levied on primary energy, which represents only one part of the cost of delivered energy (such as gasoline or electricity), and, more important, since one fuel can in many cases be substituted for another, overall price increases may not be jolting. Consumers can respond to new prices by reducing energy use and buying fewer carbon-intensive products (those, for instance, that require great amounts of carbon-based fuels to produce). In addition, some of these savings could be used to buy other less carbon-intensive goods and services.

Clearly, a carbon tax creates an incentive for producers and consumers to avoid paying the tax by reducing their use of carbon-intensive fuels. Contrary to other taxed items and activities, this avoidance has social benefits—reduced energy use and reduced CO_2 emissions. Thus, declining revenues over time indicate policy success—just the opposite of what happens when tax policy seeks to maintain steady or increasing revenues.

control costs would find it cheaper to buy the permits. A variant on a full marketable permits system for CO_2 has been proposed by Representatives Jim Cooper and Mike Synar. *(See Box 2.)* [9]

COMPARING CARBON TAXES TO OTHER CO_2-CONTROL MECHANISMS

The relative cost-effectiveness of an alternative CO_2-reduction mechanism depends heavily on how comprehensive it is vis-à-vis carbon sources and how flexible it is vis-à-vis the selection of the least expensive emissions reductions. These two factors are important for any pollution-control strategy, but especially so for a defense against carbon dioxide build-up because the individual contributing sources of CO_2 are so numerous. Taxes and marketable permits rely on flexible and diverse market responses to reduce emissions. As a result, the least costly reductions are usually undertaken first. By contrast, regulations (such as fuel-use requirements) dictate choices

or at least minimum choices that might not otherwise be made in the market.[10] Because they do not give producers and consumers much flexibility to adopt alternative control options, regulations rarely help industries identify the most inexpensive reductions. Further, regulations are unlikely to be comprehensive: in the case of CO_2 emission sources, for example, the regulatory structure would have to be overwhelmingly complex to cover all fossil fuel uses.

The potential cost savings of economic-based CO_2 control strategies, compared to those possible with command-and-control approaches, are likely to be significant. Past attempts to project the savings from proposed economic incentives suggest that command-and-control methods might cost 100 percent more than the most cost-effective tactic. Actual savings, of course, may be lower simply because no incentive scheme is perfectly designed or applied.

There is not yet a firm basis for empirically assessing the cost savings from using a carbon tax to reduce CO_2 instead of a traditional regulatory

---

BOX 2: THE COPE PROPOSAL

Representatives Jim Cooper and Mike Synar have introduced legislation designed to limit U.S. emissions of carbon dioxide. The CO_2 Offsets Policy Efficiency Act of 1991 (COPE) (H.R.2663) establishes an "emissions trading" framework under which new sources of carbon dioxide have to be offset by reductions in greenhouse emissions elsewhere in the economy. In essence, each new ton of CO_2 emitted must, under this act, be offset by a comparable reduction in CO_2 from another source.

COPE's reach and impact depends on several factors. First, COPE applies only to new sources of CO_2, though it does require that all existing utility boilers obtain offsets as they turn 65 years old. CO_2 reductions are therefore likely to occur later under COPE than they would under a carbon tax. Second, COPE addresses only emissions from sources that generate more than 100,000 tons of CO_2 per year, so the initial scope of the proposal is more limited than that typically associated with a carbon tax—an impediment to generating the lowest-cost CO_2 reductions.

The legislation also defines a broad set of sources or categories of greenhouse gases that can be

used as CO_2 offsets. While EPA could add or subtract, examples from the initial legislative list illustrate the kinds of offsets permissible:

- fuel switching from high-carbon to low-carbon fuels
- carbon sequestration from tree-planting programs
- improved motor-vehicle efficiency
- improved appliance efficiency
- methane recovery from landfills or coal mines
- increased generating efficiency and destruction of CFCs.

Under guidelines and counting rules that EPA will establish, new sources of CO_2 could pursue any of these activities to meet offset requirements. Many of these means of reducing CO_2 emissions would be encouraged by a carbon tax, though few carbon tax proposals have explicitly included offsets or deductions from the tax for tree planting or for reducing methane or CFCs.[11] Including potential offsets would certainly broaden the base for cost-effective carbon reduction.

---

approach. (All of the cost studies conducted to date assume that a carbon tax is the control strategy.) Nevertheless, the studies reviewed by Tom Tietenberg of Colby College suggest substantial potential.[12]

Under ideal circumstances, both carbon taxes and marketable permits would reduce CO_2 by the same amount at the same cost. But, as applied to CO_2 emission reduction, taxes may offer significant advantages over control strategies that focus on quantity rather than the price of emissions. Comprehensiveness and flexibility are two. But, three others—administrative costs, certainty of reductions, and adjustment costs—are equally important.[13]

Comprehensiveness

If a carbon tax were applied to each fuel at its point of production or importation into the United States, it would influence most of the fuel choices of producers and consumers of carbon-based fuels. If imported energy-intensive goods were also taxed according to roughly how much carbon was involved in their production, the tax's coverage would be even more comprehensive. The tax would initially fall, however, on the comparatively few economic actors involved at this early stage in energy production.

A permit system could also be imposed at the point of fuel production or the fuels' entry into the economy. But permit systems limited to particular fuels or sectors could actually increase emissions from uncontrolled fuels or sectors since reducing demand for fuels in controlled sectors tends to lower fuel prices in uncontrolled sectors even as permit costs make them higher in the controlled sector. A permit system might also be difficult to extend to cover imports.

Flexibility

Unlike most regulatory programs, permit systems and pollution taxes can both be adapted to changing market conditions, and both allow the least expensive reduction options to be undertaken first (provided that they achieve complete coverage of the different CO_2 sources.) A carbon tax, however, could have one advantage here over a permit system. Specifically, it may be easier to adjust the level of the tax (and, thus, emission reductions) to new information on costs and benefits. With a carbon tax,

increasing the level of control involves raising the carbon tax rate. For a permit system, it involves reducing the number of permits available or the amount of emissions covered by each permit—potentially much more difficult politically. Once allocated, permits will be viewed as a form of wealth or private property, and reducing the emissions allowed under each permit would reduce the value of the permits.

Administrative Costs

The cost-effectiveness of any market-based approach to controlling CO_2 emissions can be eroded if administrative costs are too high. Certainly, a carbon tax would entail a new collection burden for tax authorities, but entirely new entities would not be needed to impose, implement, or enforce the tax code changes. Indeed, virtually all of the data needed on fossil fuel consumption for tax purposes is already collected by various agencies. A permit system, in contrast, would require the development of a new market in CO_2 permits. (A market for SO_2 permits covering some of the same emission sources as CO_2 is already developing under the Clean Air Act Amendments of 1990. For CO_2 permits, however, the market would involve a much larger number of entities if the system is to be comprehensive.) New enforcement authorities and mechanisms would also have to be developed.

A carbon tax would entail a new collection burden for tax authorities, but entirely new entities would not be needed to impose, implement, or enforce the tax code changes. Virtually all of the data needed on fossil fuel consumption for tax purposes is already collected by various agencies.

Certainty of Reductions

Comprehensive regulatory and permit systems create relative certainty concerning the ultimate level of emissions reductions. Setting specific emissions-reduction targets and—in the case of a marketable permit strategy—fixing the number of permits allows officials to fix the amount of emissions generated, even if underlying political or economic conditions change. In contrast, a carbon tax fixes the price and lets the quantity of emissions change as producers and consumers adjust to the new price.

Does the relative uncertainty of emission reductions associated with a tax favor a marketable permit type approach to CO_2 reductions, as some analysts suggest? In the context of dealing with climate change risks, the trade-off between lower control costs and somewhat less certainty over year-to-year CO_2 emission levels can be justified. Neither the costs nor the benefits of reducing human-caused climate change can be calculated with certainty. Typically, economists argue that taxes make more sense than alternative control strategies that directly limit pollution levels when the potential economic risks are high (if also uncertain) compared to the environmental risks. Conversely, controlling quantities of pollution makes more sense when the potential environmental risks (even if uncertain) are greater compared to the economic costs. According to this logic, policies appropriate for highly toxic or acutely dangerous environmental contaminants may not be as reasonable in efforts to minimize climate change.

The risks of climate change are real, but they are not as immediate as the potential costs of control. Yet, economic risks have to be accepted today to avoid potentially significant environmental risks in the future. Prudent public policy dictates a control strategy with near-term economic risks that can be easily managed.[14]

With tax-based mitigation programs, the economic costs of CO_2 reductions can be minimized. This tack would mean greater uncertainty in the short term over the ultimate environmental outcome, but it would not preclude switching course if additional information that alters the relative importance of the costs and benefits of climate change becomes available.

Adjustment Costs

All of the CO_2-reduction strategies give rise to economic inefficiencies as producers and consumers adjust to changing prices. A regulatory reduction strategy is likely to have the largest adjustment costs because it is rigid and because response opportunities are fewer. A carbon tax or permit system would have similar adjustment costs if they were similarly comprehensive. But because a permit system is quantity-based, the permit price may fluctuate over time, possibly requiring multiple new adjustments. Uncertain prices can themselves add to the overall cost of emission reductions. With a carbon tax, emission quantities may fluctuate within a general downward trend, as noted, but the overall price certainty can help the economy adjust to the controls by sending consistent signals to producers and consumers. (The possible range adjustment costs associated with a carbon tax are discussed in the next section. There are no comparable estimates for regulatory or permit-based systems.)

CARBON TAXES AND OPPORTUNITIES FOR TAX REFORM

The economic advantages of carbon taxes, as compared to both command-and-control responses to climate change and to marketable permits, are substantial. But the relative cost of control is not the only advantage. The revenues produced by a carbon tax could have a much broader impact on our economic well-being: carbon taxes and other pollution taxes offer a basis for reforming our current tax system. Carbon tax revenues can be used to shift the economic burden of our current tax to encourage "goods," such as investments in capital and labor, and to discourage "bads," such as air pollution, thereby promoting longer-term economic growth and a healthier economy.[15]

Taxes allow for the provision of public services by shifting production from private to public goods. By changing the relative prices paid by consumers and producers, they also change the way resources are used.[16] When the income from investment in new capital is taxed, for instance, less capital will be used to produce goods and services and, as a result, productivity will fall. The same is true of taxes on labor income. The loss in output of goods and services that results is referred to as the distortionary impact of the tax or its "deadweight loss." Because of this phenomenon, for every dollar raised in tax revenues, more than a dollar's worth of private production is lost.

The size of the deadweight loss varies, depending upon what is being taxed (capital, labor, resources, final goods, etc.) and the marginal tax rate. In general, deadweight loss increases as the marginal tax rate rises. Even after the tax reforms of 1986, the average cost to the economy was an estimated 18 cents for every dollar of tax revenue raised.[17] Thus, if this estimate were applicable to federal tax revenues in 1990, which totalled roughly 1.1 trillion dollars from all sources, the loss in economic efficiency in 1990 from the existing tax system was around $200 billion dollars. Of course, the total economic loss would be even greater if state tax revenues—some $800 billion in 1990—were also included from personal and corporate income taxes, indirect business taxes, and payroll taxes.[18]

As might be expected, and as Table 2 shows, the marginal costs of raising each new dollar by taxing conventional "goods" are much higher than the average burden across all dollars raised. While the estimates of efficiency loss vary according to the assumptions reflected in the various models and the model structure, they tell a similar story. Each additional dollar from all tax sources costs the economy anywhere from 21 cents to 46 cents, according to these results. The largest burdens appear to result from taxes on capital and corporate or individual incomes. Jorgenson and Yun estimate that for every additional dollar raised through capital income taxes, the economy loses 92 cents in lost economic productivity.

Table 2 makes a compelling economic case for reforming the tax system to take advantage of the lower deadweight loss of different tax bases. For example, raising one dollar less from capital income taxes and replacing it with a dollar from a sales tax would save the economy 57 cents. (As discussed in Section 3, tax choices also raise income distribution issues.)

When the revenues generated by a pollution tax are used to reduce the marginal tax rates on capital, labor, and other resources, the deadweight loss from these taxes is also reduced. For this reason, a carbon tax can be viewed as eliminating an existing distortion rather than creating a new one. Although any pollution option will result in shifts in how resources are used, which may in time reduce economic performance, the opportunity to reduce other tax rates

Table 2. Estimated Loss in Economic Efficiency from Alternative Forms of Taxation

Taxes	Marginal	Average
All Taxes	0.460	0.212
Corporate Income Taxes	0.838	0.614
Capital Income Taxes, Individual and Corporate	0.924	0.674
Property Taxes	0.174	0.158
Labor Income Tax	0.482	0.295
Sales Tax	0.256	0.228
Individual Income Tax	0.598	0.333

Source: Jorgenson, Dale W. and Kun-Young Yun. "The Excess Burden of Taxation in the U.S.," HIER Discussion Paper No. 1528, Harvard University, Cambridge, MA, November 1990.

creates a countervailing tendency to increase economic growth. Because current marginal tax rates on capital and labor income are very high (on the order of 30 percent) relative to taxes on raw materials (such as fossil fuels), at least for a moderate level of a carbon tax the overall effect on GNP will probably be positive.

The actual dollar gain to the economy of reforming the tax system by substituting a carbon tax for some portion of existing tax depends on how big the tax offset is and on which tax or taxes are reduced. The revenue implications of a carbon tax designed to merely stabilize CO_2 emissions suggest that the benefit could be substantial. If, for example, $35 billion in carbon tax revenues were used to reduce corporate income taxes by the same amount, the economy would be better off by between $23 billion and $32 billion.[19]

An increasing number of carbon tax studies (many of which are reviewed in the next section) show the economic benefits of reducing the burden of our tax system. Yet, many analysts also argue that the potential tax-reform benefits of pollution taxes should not be included in an assessment of carbon tax policies and that a carbon tax must be fully justified on the basis of environmental risk alone.[20] Their point is that the uses to which the revenues of the

> *The fact that pollution taxes can form the basis for tax reform benefits is a major comparative advantage.*

tax could be put and the economic benefits of doing so constitute a separate policy issue. But to ignore the economic implications of how the potentially significant revenues generated by a carbon tax are used is to provide a less than complete picture of the economic and environmental characteristics of a carbon tax strategy. Indeed, the fact that pollution taxes can form the basis for tax reform benefits is a major comparative advantage.[21]

SETTING THE RIGHT LEVEL OF A CARBON TAX

The higher the cost of fossil fuels, the less they will be used to produce goods and services, and the less carbon dioxide will be released into the atmosphere as a result. But how much reduction is enough? How big should a carbon tax be? If environmental considerations alone are the measure, the ideal tax rate is one set at the point at which the benefits from the last ton of carbon removed equal the added cost of eliminating that ton. But this point is notoriously difficult to find, especially for benefits that may be many generations in the future or for situations in which the science or relative risks are not completely understood. This number cannot be calculated until emissions are translated into atmospheric concentrations (concentrations, not levels of emissions, determine the warming effect of CO_2); until the effects of increased concentrations on the rate and level of warming are estimated; until the environmental and economic impacts or injuries associated with the warming are assessed, and until a dollar value is placed on the estimated damages. As is the case for many pollutants, researchers simply don't know enough yet to perform the initial calculations.

Preliminary efforts have been made to assign a dollar value to a small set of potential environmental risks associated with climate change, including loss in agricultural production. The most widely quoted of these estimates finds economic damages from a doubling of atmospheric CO_2 concentrations in the range of 0.5 percent of GNP for the United States.[22] But early estimates like these must still be considered largely speculative. They are also likely to be conservative since many categories of potential environmental loss that could far outweigh more direct economic losses have yet to be quantified at all. For instance, some scientific consensus is forming that damages to unique or particularly sensitive ecosystems from rapid climate change constitute especially important environmental risks, but no damage estimates take their potential economic costs into account.

> *The ideal tax rate is one set at the point at which the benefits from the last ton of carbon removed equal the added cost of eliminating that ton.*

In a more recent analysis of the economic damages in the U.S. from climate change, William Cline suggests that more inclusive estimates may be in the range of one to two percent of U.S. gross domestic product, or around $60–$117 billion annually.[23] Cline also notes that these estimates do not consider the economic losses associated with atmospheric CO_2 concentrations that go beyond a twofold increase, even though atmospheric concentrations would almost certainly pass the doubling point if no efforts are made to reduce CO_2 emissions. He estimates economic damages from global warming in their very long-term to be around six percent of U.S. G.D.P. or approximately $340 billion annually.

The lack of formal data on the degree to which market prices fail to reflect environmental damages is not unique to greenhouse warming. But a shortage of data on various other environmental problems does not stop the development of programs to reduce risks. More generally, many types of federal and state excise taxes are justified in part as ways to raise the price of certain goods to reflect the social costs associated with their consumption. But such "sin" taxes (on alcohol or tobacco, for example) are rarely set on the basis of a formal accounting of the social costs and benefits of reducing the use of the taxed product.

The most common alternative method of determining the size of a carbon tax is to estimate the tax level necessary to achieve a pre-selected level of CO_2 emissions. For example, a tax can be chosen to stabilize emissions at 1990 levels by the year 2000. (This approach is used in a current legislative proposal. *See Box 3.*) A carbon tax set on this basis is likely to be consistent with the terms of any international agreement on climate change risks and with the way both environmental regulations and permits are set. This approach avoids the difficulties associated with explicit assessments of economic damages from climate change that include specific CO_2-reduction targets. It

does raise other concerns, however. Most prominent among these is that the "right" tax is difficult to establish with certainty in advance and depends on the time frame selected and the level of control required. The tax necessary to stabilize emissions at one level in the year 2000 may be very different from a tax that stabilizes emissions at another in the year 2010 or 2020. This is not just an academic concern. Virtually all economic analyses of carbon-reduction possibilities suggest that substantial early reductions, say over the next 10 or 15 years, can be achieved quite inexpensively. If so, a fairly low tax would be sufficient if levied soon. But as time goes on, keeping or extending these reductions may become harder and harder, requiring a significantly higher tax. Eventually, of course, alternatives to fossil fuels are likely to become available, which would lower the required tax rate.

BOX 3: THE STARK CARBON TAX PROPOSAL

Representative Stark (D.CA.) has introduced a proposal that illustrates the basic concepts of a carbon tax. H.R. 1086 is based roughly on a carbon tax option prepared by the Congressional Budget Office (CBO). It calls for a phased-in tax of $30 per ton of carbon in coal, oil and natural gas. According to the Congressional Budget Office, a tax of this magnitude

might stabilize emissions of CO_2 at current levels by the year 2000. (This assessment does not assume a phased-in tax schedule.) Table 3 presents the proposed tax rate by fuel type for the phase-in period. In Table 4, these rates are expressed as the estimated percentage increase in the price of the taxed fuels. H.R. 1086 keeps the real tax rate fixed by allowing it to rise with the rate of inflation.

Table 3. Proposed Carbon Tax Schedule of H.R. 1086

	Carbon ($/Ton)	Coal ($/Ton)	Oil ($/Brl)	Nat. Gas ($/TCF)	Estimated Revenue ($ Bill)
Year 1	6	3.60	0.77	0.10	7
Year 2	12	7.20	1.54	0.19	14
Year 3	18	10.80	2.31	0.30	21
Year 4	24	14.40	3.09	0.40	28
Year 5	30	18.00	3.85	0.48	36

Source: World Resources Institute.

Table 4. Estimated Affect on Fuel Prices of H.R. 1086 Carbon Tax Proposal

Tax as a % of Production Price	Coal	Oil	Natural Gas
Year 1	16	4	4
Year 2	31	8	8
Year 3	47	12	12
Year 4	63	16	16
Year 5	78	19	19

Source: World Resources Institute.

III. ESSENTIAL ELEMENTS OF A CARBON TAX STRATEGY

A carefully designed carbon tax can create significant environmental and economic benefits. A poorly designed and implemented one will generate few benefits and can impose substantial costs. An effective domestic carbon tax strategy—that is, a tax program that captures the economic and environmental benefits discussed earlier without unduly hurting any single sector of the economy—must meet three general conditions:

1. minimizing the short-term economic losses by careful use of the revenues;
2. maximizing the economic returns by lowering other tax rates; and
3. compensating groups adversely affected.

All three are essential to its economic, environmental, and political success.

ECONOMIC CONSEQUENCES OF CARBON TAXES

A properly set pollution tax generates net gains in overall social welfare from the environmental improvements it creates, regardless of its fiscal implications or its impact on official GNP estimates. Nonetheless, concerns about the economic consequences of a tax abide. Because the environmental justification for a carbon tax is that the benefits are worth the costs associated with the policy, policy-makers must have a good idea of what these costs are likely to be. They need to know the potential impact of a carbon tax on the production of goods and services, as well as who pays or bears the burden of the tax.

Macroeconomic Impacts of Carbon Taxes

Numerous studies have estimated the macroeconomic consequences of carbon taxes designed to reduce CO_2 emissions to various levels. The studies differ significantly in both approach and results, but most models suggest that the economic consequences are likely to be either fairly small losses or outright gains.[24]

As Table 5 shows, a carbon tax will alter the use of capital, labor, energy, and other economic resources.

Since a carbon tax makes fossil fuels more expensive, businesses and households will search for ways to lower their tax payments by reducing their use of fossil fuels and increasing their use of capital, labor, and non-fossil energy. Consumers might respond to higher electric prices by buying more efficient appliances or using the ones they have less. Utilities might increasingly make electricity with energy sources that emit little or no carbon (biomass and wind or solar power). The net effect of these switches is that the production of some goods and services will fall. The fall in overall GNP projected in some models reflects the impact of these changes on overall market prices and household expenditures.

The way the revenues from the carbon tax are used further changes the picture. The ranges presented in Table 5 represent the impact of different revenue recycling options. In two of the studies in Table 5, the revenues are recycled by reducing the tax rate on capital or labor. These tax changes reduce the price of using capital and labor and thus potentially improve economic performance. The projected economic advantages from the revenue recycling more than compensate for any direct GNP loss associated with the carbon tax.

The range of carbon taxes analyzed in these studies—from $17/ton to $500/ton—appears at first glance to be too broad to be much help in determining the economic consequences of controlling CO_2 emissions. Interestingly, however, the estimated range of impacts on GNP is much smaller, from a loss of 3 percent to a gain of 1 percent, as compared to what GNP would be without the tax, and it does not rise in lock step with the carbon tax rate. In dollar terms, this amounts to a maximum loss of about $164 billion based on 1990 GNP to a possible gain of $55 billion.

Table 6 presents the results of studies that consider a wider array of estimated macroeconomic impacts from carbon taxes, including inflation and unemployment. The range of results within each study reflect multiple uses of the same model with different assumptions about how the tax dollars are recycled.

Table 5. Estimates of the Macroeconomic Cost of Reducing Carbon Dioxide Emissions Through a Carbon Tax: General Equilibrium & Optimization Models

Study	Carbon Reductions (%Δ from baseline)	Carbon Tax Rate ($/ton carbon)	Recycling Revenues	Change in GNP (%Δ from baseline)
Shackleton, et al./D-GEM	2020 = 80% of 1990	$40	No	– 1.6
		$40	Yes	– 0.7 to 1
Shackleton, et al./Goulder	2020 = 80% of 1990	$40	No	– 2.4
		$40	Yes	– 2.2 to – 0.3
CBO/Edmonds-Reilly	> 20% cut by 2100	100	No	– 1
Bradley et al./Fossil 2	2000 = 80% of 1990	~ $500	No	– 1.3
	2030 = 80% of 1990	$300		– 0.7
	2000 = 1990	$100		< – 1
Manne, Richels/ETA-MACRO	2000 = 1990; 2020 = 80% of 1990	$250	No	– 3
Jorgenson & Wilcoxen/D-GEM	2020 = 1990	$17	No	– 0.5
	2020 = 80% of 1990	$60	No	– 1.6

Sources: Jorgenson, Dale W. and Peter Wilcoxen, *Reducing U.S. Carbon Emissions: The Cost of Different Goals,* Center for Science & International Affairs, JFK School of Government, Harvard, Oct. 1991; Bradley, Richard A., Edward C. Watts, & Edward R. Williams, *Limiting Net Greenhouse Gas Emissions in the United States,* U.S. Department of Energy, December 1991; Manne, A. & Richard G. Richels, "CO$_2$ Emission Limits: An Economic Cost Analysis for the USA, The Energy Journal, Vol. 11, No. 2 (April 1990); Congressional Budget Office, *Carbon Charges as a Response to Global Warming: The Effects of Taxing Fossil Fuels,* August 1991; Shackleton, Robert et. al., "The Efficiency Value of Carbon Tax Revenues," Draft December 16, 1991.

The positive estimated impacts on GNP reflect tax recycling options which promote efficiency improvements in the economy. These studies include the short-run costs to the economy of adjusting to the new tax. Since consumers and producers must adjust their current activities to account for the new fossil fuel prices for a time, resources might not be used as productively as possible, particularly since some adjustments may be hard to make quickly. Thermostats can be turned up or down almost immediately without extra costs, but buying a new, more energy-efficient car will be costly if it means retiring the old one early. Such adjustment costs are not unique to carbon taxes—they can occur whenever prices rise or fall, as they did when oil prices dropped several

years ago—and they may lead to unemployment and inflation. (Estimates of unemployment and inflation associated with these adjustments are highly sensitive to assumptions about changes in monetary policy in response to the tax.[25]) But their effects on GNP will not be permanent.

The studies presented in Table 6 do not reflect as wide a range of carbon taxes as those included in Table 5. In dollar terms, the range is bounded by annual losses of around $109 billion at one extreme to a gain of $207 billion at the other if they occurred today.

The studies available to date suggest several preliminary observations in comparing the results identified in Tables 5 and 6. One study in Table 6 does

Table 6. Estimates of the Macroeconomic Costs of Reducing CO_2 Emissions Through a Carbon Tax

Study	Carbon Reductions (%Δ from baseline)	Carbon Tax Rate ($/ton carbon)	Recycling Revenues	Change in GNP (%Δ from baseline)	Unemployment	Inflation
EIA/DRI quarterly	unspecified	$40	Yes	− 07% to − 0.8%		1.7%
CBO/DRI quarterly	6% below 2000	$100	No	− 2%	0.15	1%
Shackleton, et al./ DRI quarterly	2.5–6.0	$40	Yes	− 1% to 3.75%		
Shackleton, et al./ Wharton	0–7.0	$40	Yes	− 0.4% to 3.8%		

Sources: EIA, *Studies of Energy Taxes,* Service Report SR/EMEU/91-02, April 1991; Congressional Budget Office, *Carbon Charges as a Response to Global Warming: The Effects of Taxing Fossil Fuels,* August 1991; Shackleton, Robert, et. al., ''The Efficiency Value of Carbon Tax Revenues,'' Draft December 16, 1991.

not involve revenue recycling.[26] Compared to the $100 a ton carbon taxes analyzed in Table 5, the GNP losses are somewhat higher, as would be expected. The three studies in Table 6 that involve revenue recycling generate larger GNP gains (and in one case a smaller GNP) than the two $40 per ton taxes analyzed in Table 5. The reasons for this are not immediately clear, though the inclusion of short-run stimuli from the tax cuts in the Table 6 models may be the cause.

Understanding the Model Results

Even though the estimates from models of the economic impacts associated with using a carbon tax to control global warming vary, the results suggest what the contours of an effective carbon tax strategy might be. For perspective, though, remember that a negative macroeconomic result from a pollution tax is not equivalent to a true economic or welfare loss. To be sure, any estimated reduction in the amount of goods and services produced that stems from a pollution tax is a cost. But without some notion of the offsetting environmental benefits of the same tax, it's impossible to know whether on balance we, as a society, are better or worse off.

Where the Tax Revenues Go

The large revenue streams generated by a carbon tax can have economic effects much larger than those triggered by changes in relative prices. Such impacts will vary, depending on how the revenues are used. The studies presented in Tables 5 and 6 take two different approaches toward handling carbon tax revenues. They either (1) return the revenues to consumers in lump-sum reimbursements or (2) reinvest them to promote economic growth by cutting the marginal tax ratio. (The latter option has been aptly called ''recycling the revenues.'')

Raising energy prices through a carbon tax without considering any other actions—a so-called lump-sum distribution—does lower economic performance (lower GNP): carbon-intensive inputs and products are squeezed out of the economy by what were once considered less valuable (and less carbon-intensive) inputs and products. As a result, the economy cannot grow as fast and as quickly as it otherwise would.

Tables 5 and 6 make it clear, however, that reinvesting or recycling the tax revenues into the economy by lowering payroll or capital tax rates can, at a minimum, offset a significant portion of any estimated loss in GNP. In four out of five cases, carefully targeted tax reductions result in a projected GNP that stays the same or rises relative to what it would have been without the carbon tax. These results are consistent with the relatively large deadweight losses associated with existing tax rates on capital and labor. More important, the economic gains from reducing existing deadweight loss outweigh any economic losses associated with reduced fossil fuel use. GNP losses in studies where tax revenues are recycled either don't fully capture the tax-reform gains or evaluate specific types of tax cuts that have little economic impact.

Even models that don't conclude that the full effect of a carbon tax on GNP is positive show that economic impacts are significantly reduced. In a 1991 (Energy Information Administration, Department of Energy) study of energy taxes, for example, the revenues from a carbon tax were used to reduce the payroll tax rate paid by employers and employees. As a result, the net present value of GNP losses over a ten-year period attributable to a $40 per ton carbon tax were reduced from $226 billion with no offset to $23 billion with an offset—a 90-percent reduction.[27] Of various options for using carbon tax

revenues, only a lump-sum reimbursement, simply giving all consumers back a portion of the tax, fails to improve economic productivity. This approach might stimulate some short-term consumer spending, but it does nothing to overcome the basic inefficiencies of the existing tax code and therefore to contribute to long-run economic improvement.

Estimates generated by one model of the impact on GNP of a carbon tax coupled with different uses of the revenues appear in Figure 1. As the figure shows, GNP losses fall by 50 percent or more if revenues are recycled instead of distributed on a lump-sum basis. Recycling revenues by cutting taxes on capital brings GNP above what it would have been in the absence of the tax. In this figure, positive GNP results indicate that the economic advantages of reducing existing tax burdens through tax shifting alone are sufficient to justify a carbon tax.

Different models yield different answers to the question of which use of the carbon tax revenues would have the largest GNP benefit. Nonetheless, any productive application of the revenues is clearly preferable from a GNP perspective to lump-sum redistributions, and the positive GNP estimates associated with revenue recycling impart a better sense

Figure I. Impact of Alternative Tax Recycling Assumptions on Estimated Gross National Product From A Carbon Tax

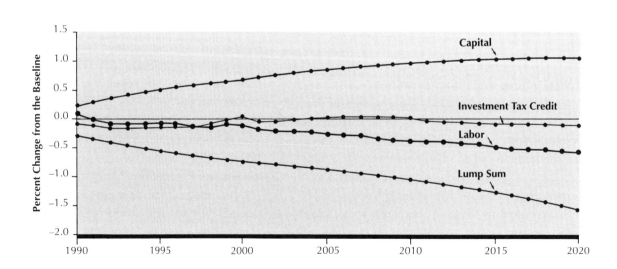

Source: R. Shackleton, et al., "The Efficiency Value of Carbon Tax Revenues," U.S. Environmental Protection Agency, Washington, D.C. (March 1992)

of the potential macroeconomic implications of carbon taxes than the negative estimates do.

Flexibility in Responding to the Tax

The full range of energy production and consumption decisions, large and small, will determine how fossil fuel use and carbon emissions change under a carbon tax. In models, everything else being equal, the more thoroughly the various economic choices are portrayed in the models, the more accurate the resulting macroeconomic estimates. Ideally, macroeconomic models would reflect all of these choices, but some are much more inclusive than others. Dale Jorgenson and Peter Wilcoxen of Harvard University and the University of Texas, respectively, for example, include equations and mathematical relationships that describe many of the choices outlined above for many different industries and household types. As a result, energy markets respond more readily and with more variety to price signals in their analysis. This is a key point since, in general, the availability of more choices and options means that smaller carbon taxes are required to reduce carbon emissions to any given levels. (For the record, the Jorgenson-Wilcoxen model has been criticized for being overly flexible in the way consumers and producers respond to price changes, in part because capital stocks are readily transformed to other uses [*see,* for example, CBO, 1990]. Although this is a limitation in the short run, over time capital stocks do turn over and are not a limiting factor in responding to the tax.)

Other models limit the possible range of economic choices. The Fossil 2 model used by Richard Bradley and his colleagues at the Department of Energy, for example, does not allow consumers and producers to replace operating equipment with equipment that is more efficient or that uses alternative fuels. In the case of automobiles, where capital stock turns over relatively quickly anyway, this limitation doesn't matter greatly. But in the case of buildings or utilities, where substantial fuel-switching and retrofit opportunities are excluded, it does. Not surprisingly, the Bradley study finds that very high taxes and economic impacts are needed to achieve near-term emission reductions.

Recent history shows that energy markets can be more responsive to energy prices than many forecasters

have suggested and that carbon reductions may cost less. Precisely because energy markets involve so many decision-points, economic analyses of carbon taxes must be based on models that incorporate as many of the key economic choices and opportunities as possible.

Recent history shows that energy markets can be more responsive to energy prices than many forecasters have suggested and that carbon reductions may cost less.

Energy Use and the Economy

All of the models included in Tables 5 and 6 specify how energy use affects economic productivity and, therefore, opportunities to produce goods and services. There are two basic approaches to creating this link. Most of the models listed in Table 5 describe the detailed relationships among energy use, productivity, and consumer choices. The model itself determines what impact changes in the energy sector have on the overall economy. Some of the models listed in Table 6, on the other hand, are relatively "hard wired"—that is, they tie productivity and economic growth largely to the amount of energy used. In effect, these models assume that if energy use falls because of higher energy prices, the economy must be worse off. Bradley and his colleagues tested the importance of this hard-wiring and found that when one particular macroeconomic model is run with the assumption that efficiency improvements can improve overall productivity, estimated GNP losses can fall by half.[28] In general, the more well-defined the link between energy use and economic activity, the lower the estimated cost of a carbon tax.

There are certainly other ways in which the models differ—baseline projections of population and economic growth are two—but these three aspects of energy-economic modeling stand out as key to interpreting the model results for policy-makers.

What the Models Don't Tell Us

The model results in Tables 5 and 6 share some common elements. In particular, all of the models may overstate the potential GNP losses (or underestimate the gains) of a carbon tax in three ways. First, the potential for cost-effective efficiency-investment opportunities are largely overlooked. Virtually all the models assume that producers and consumers are taking advantage of all cost-effective energy savings opportunities at current energy prices. If so, energy prices cannot change without forcing individuals or firms to make changes that cost more than if the tax had not been imposed. Yet, institutional constraints, transaction costs, and regulatory barriers, for example, may keep energy users from taking full advantage of energy-saving opportunities at observed prices. Indeed, studies based on the costs and benefits of specific energy-efficiency and alternative-energy investments suggest that very large CO_2 emissions cuts could be made that would generate positive economic returns.[29] Investments in energy-efficient lighting, motors, and other appliances, for instance, can often generate savings in electricity demand at half the cost of developing new power plants. Since none of the macroeconomic models reviewed here allow for such possibilities, they are likely to inflate adjustment costs and economic losses.

These "bottom-up" analyses, which attempt to fully describe the technical opportunities for energy savings do not directly analyze a specific policy proposal (such as a carbon tax), and they don't generate GNP estimates from the cost-effective investments examined. Even if they did, a carbon tax alone would not realize all of the cost-effective carbon savings included in these studies. (Increasing energy prices would not, for instance, remove regulatory barriers to energy efficiency investments, though investments prompted by the tax are likely to induce many of these cost-effective alternatives, thus lowering economic costs and possibly resulting in net economic gains.) The potential for cost-effective alternatives to using more energy are not directly reflected in any of the models included in Tables 5 and 6. While projected increases in energy demand (the baseline of the models) may be adjusted to include energy efficiency improvements, none of these are directly related to using energy prices associated

with the carbon tax. But sensitivity analyses in several of the studies in Table 5 show that faster improvements in energy efficiency can reduce projected impacts on GNP by more than half even if the effects of recycling revenues back to the economy by lowering tax burdens aren't considered.[30]

Second, the benefits from a carbon tax other than those related to climate are not included in the GNP estimates presented in Tables 5 and 6. Chief among these are the reduction in non-carbon pollution associated with using less fossil fuel and the national security benefits of using less imported fuel. If less oil, gas, and coal were burned, there would be less sulfur dioxide (SO_2), nitrogen oxides (NO_x), and other air-borne emissions in the atmosphere, as well as fewer land, ocean, and groundwater impacts from developing and moving the fuels. Estimates of the social cost of importing oil, estimates based on the risks of economic disruption, range from $0 to $10 per barrel.[31] The EIA study mentioned earlier pegs the national security benefits of a $40/ton carbon tax total around $18.1 billion. A full analysis of the economic costs of a carbon tax would account for these secondary benefits and for their effect on the manufacture and use of goods and services.

Finally, price signals stimulate technological change, accelerating the development of new efficiency options and non-fossil energy supplies and decreasing their costs. All of the models reflect some technological improvement over time based on historical trends. But only one (Jorgenson/Wilcoxen) factors in the potential impact of price changes on technological change, and even in this model, specific energy-efficiency and renewable options do not change as a result of the tax policy—a significant omission in the case of a carbon tax, particularly as time passes. Indeed, the cost differential between fossil fuels and non-fossil alternatives is a major determinant of the cost of meeting a CO_2 emission-reduction goal and, thus, of the size of the tax; price changes would accelerate technological development and narrow this gap. Sensitivity analysis using different assumed costs of future non-fossil technologies only partially and indirectly addresses this aspect of carbon taxes.

Figure 2 illustrates the cost implications of carbon taxes when three of the factors described here—tax recycling, cost-effective opportunities, and non-climate benefits—are included in the analysis. Studies that exclude these three considerations will report GNP losses that grow with the size of carbon tax. But when these three other elements are taken into account, the potential for economic gain, in addition to that associated with climate benefits, rises.

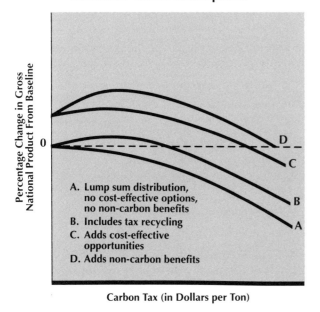

Figure 2. Impact of a Carbon Tax on Estimated Gross National Product Under Alternative Economic Model Assumptions

A. Lump sum distribution, no cost-effective options, no non-carbon benefits
B. Includes tax recycling
C. Adds cost-effective opportunities
D. Adds non-carbon benefits

Carbon Tax (in Dollars per Ton)

Source: Adapted from J. Sweeney, Personal Notes, Stanford University, Stanford, California

Implications of Macroeconomic Modeling Results

Although no modeling efforts fully incorporate all of the elements discussed above, a carbon tax strategy (including tax revenue recycling) makes economic sense, especially when existing cost-effective efficiency options and non-climate benefits are taken into account. Naturally, if the benefits associated with reducing climate instability are considered, carbon taxes look even better.

Besides providing a picture of the economic impacts of a carbon tax, the studies evaluated here suggest several policy-related conclusions:

1. Certain types of production and consumption responses to a carbon tax will come into play only after the tax has been in effect for some years. (Large-scale shifts in technology are an obvious example.) Some models capture various points in the slow process of change in response to a carbon tax

better than others. For example, the Data Resources, Inc. macroeconomic model has a fairly short-run orientation and offers a quite useful picture of the early economic adjustments associated with a carbon tax, but is weaker vis-à-vis long-term adjustments involving changes in capital stock. On the other hand, the Jorgenson/Wilcoxen model focuses exclusively on the long run. Given the various strengths of various models, policy-makers should not rely heavily on any single set of model results to gauge all the economic effects of a carbon tax. Rather, several models representing different points or spans in time should be used.

2. Emissions reductions can be achieved relatively cheaply in the near term, but the economic impacts can grow over time. Most of the models, as well as other analyses, agree that early reductions are relatively inexpensive, though they may disagree on the point at which costs start to rise. The Manne-Richels model, for instance, concluded that a tax of $250 a ton is required for long-term emissions reductions; but that same study also concludes that over the first decade or so the tax could be set at only $29 per ton to achieve similar reductions.[32]

3. The sooner CO_2 emission reductions are begun, the lower the required tax and resultant economic costs of meeting any particular target will be. Each new building, factory, or car represents a commitment to energy demand for at least ten years to come. Similarly, each new electric plant creates a commitment to a particular fuel source for decades. U.S. demand for energy services and supplies in 2040 are already being shaped by today's decisions. Unfortunately, many opportunities are being lost. These "lost opportunities" show up in modeling results as increased economic costs when the time allowed to meet any given target is compressed. Simply put, it is cheaper to reduce current emissions by 20 percent by 2010 if reductions begin in 1990 than if they begin in 2000.

4. Keeping carbon emissions at the same level will require different levels of effort from year to year, depending on underlying population and economic growth trends and the availability of efficiency investments and non-fossil alternatives. In fact, the highest reported tax rates may be needed for only a few years. In nearly all of the studies reviewed here, growth in demand for energy services begins to outstrip efficiency opportunities after a decade or two. Soon thereafter, however, newer and less expensive non-fossil energy sources become available. These technical improvements then lower the tax rate needed to induce fuel switching away from fossil fuels, and the continued availability of the alternative fuels keeps the rate low almost regardless of how much demand grows. Indeed, if nuclear or renewable energy sources turn out to be less expensive than coal-based alternatives, carbon taxes could eventually be removed altogether. At any rate, since aggregate models don't fully reflect the extent to which higher carbon prices spur technological development, it may well be that no tax spike would be needed to maintain steady reductions matched to specific targets.

5. Phasing-in taxes can reduce costs. The short-run adjustment costs discussed above arise in part because capital resources are not very flexible. Capital and technological choices are based on expected future energy prices. When prices change unexpectedly, owners of capital stock may not be able to respond quickly or well to the new price signals. When gasoline prices rise, for instance, some drivers will reduce their time on the road and buy more efficient automobiles right away, but most will take their time.

Economic adjustment imposes costs as prices and markets rearrange around the new higher prices for carbon-based fuels. It turns out, however, that adjustment costs are at least as much a factor of whether the price changes are anticipated as the overall size of the price change. One study has found that a significant fraction of the estimated productivity loss associated with the energy price increases of the 1970s was due to the unexpected temporary price spike, not the underlying gradual increases in real oil prices.[33] Simply introducing a new carbon tax without any attempt to minimize these economic impacts would be unnecessarily costly.

Revenue recycling can reduce adjustment costs, but much more can be done too. The most obvious option for managing the adjustment costs of a carbon tax, one often neglected in tax modeling, is to phase in the tax over time. Phasing in the tax allows energy consumers and producers more time to adjust to new prices. Further, if the time schedule for the tax is set out clearly, energy users can make their

economic decisions with future prices in mind. Few of the models used in carbon tax analyses reflect the assumption that expectations over future price changes can moderate economic impacts.

The H.R. 1086 carbon tax proposal calls for a five-year phase-in. In the Congressional Budget Office's carbon tax options, the high option would be put in place over ten years. Interestingly, no studies permit a side-by-side comparison of a carbon tax with and without a phase-in period. One study of different gasoline taxes, however, showed that the economic loss of a 50-cent a gallon tax can be reduced in the early years of the tax by 60 percent if the tax is introduced gradually over several years.[34]

6. Allowing carbon offsets can lower the economic costs of achieving a given level of CO_2 emission reductions. Other sources of atmospheric carbon dioxide besides fossil fuel combustion and other greenhouse gases besides carbon dioxide contribute to the risks of accelerated climate change. For example, when temperate and tropical forests are lost, vast quantities of carbon dioxide are released into the atmosphere. Methane, nitrous oxide, and certain other trace gases also add to the greenhouse effect—some are much more powerful in this regard than CO_2. Any serious strategy for reducing greenhouse risks should include these other sources and gases.

Credits or offsets against a carbon tax could be allowed when consumers or producers bring down emissions from these other gases or other sources. For example, a coal company could reduce its tax burden by planting trees that would absorb carbon dioxide and offset some portion of the emissions attributable to the combustion of its coal. Similarly, an oil company could lower its carbon tax payments by reducing methane losses from natural gas pipelines. The logic behind such proposals is solid. Reductions in any greenhouse gas (or increases in greenhouse sinks) help lower climate change risks. It makes economic sense to encourage these reductions if they can be achieved (on a carbon equivalent basis) for less than it costs to reduce CO_2 from fossil fuel combustion. Indeed, the impact of offsets on the total economic costs of a carbon-control strategy is significant.

Too little is known right now about the sources of and control options for methane emissions to make methane reduction part of a carbon tax strategy.

A recent Department of Energy study attempts to model the inclusion of a methane tax along with a carbon tax, but could not tie the tax directly to methane emissions, only to average industry-wide emission levels. Such a tax would provide no incentive for individual producers to reduce their emission levels.

Emerging data and experience with tree-planting programs, however, highlight the potential cost savings associated with broadening the carbon tax structure to include tree planting as carbon dioxide offsets.[35] Recent analyses of the costs of constructing tree-planting programs for absorbing carbon place the marginal cost per metric ton in the range of $18 to $80[36]—below many of the carbon tax rates being discussed. The total cost of bringing carbon emissions down to a given level or keeping them there could be reduced by allowing a credit or exemption from the tax for each unit of carbon sequestered through a tree-planting program. A DOE analysis suggests that the costs of a 20-percent emissions cut in greenhouse gas emissions could be reduced by 20–80 percent of what costs would have been if reforestation offsets are part of the strategy.[37]

A major selling point of a carbon tax strategy, administrative simplicity, is easily lost if performance tests, monitoring, and assessment programs get complicated.

Of course, the mechanics of creating a tax-offset program have to be carefully considered. A major selling point of a carbon tax strategy, administrative simplicity, is easily lost if performance tests, monitoring, and assessment programs get complicated. The potentially substantial benefits of offsets could themselves be offset by high management costs.

DISTRIBUTIONAL CONSEQUENCES OF CARBON TAXES

By nature, taxes—or any kind of revenue-raising measure—make some people worse off than they would have been without the tax. Indeed, as a practical matter, any form of CO_2-reduction program affects somebody's wealth. The question is whether taxes have better or worse distributional effects than a marketable permit or regulatory strategy for reducing CO_2 emissions. Unfortunately, it is impossible at this point to make a comparison between the various options since only carbon taxes have been subject to a formal distributional analysis.

It is possible, however, to highlight the wealth effects of carbon taxes beginning with the issue of fairness—a staple in the design of U.S. federal tax policy. A shaping force behind the current structure of federal taxes is the desire to impose less burden on lower-income groups relative to higher-income groups.[38] A progressive tax is typically considered more fair than one that taxes lower incomes at equal or greater rates than higher incomes. For this reason, federal receipts come mainly from income taxes that are graduated.

The perception that energy taxes are "unfair" has been perhaps the major barrier to their widespread application. The apparent regressive nature of energy taxes has been roundly criticized, though other potential distributional impacts, both regional and industrial, have also sparked concern. However large the overall economic gains from such taxes, a sound carbon tax strategy would thus have to include a program to compensate those adversely affected by the tax.

The Impact of Energy Taxes by Income Class

Conventional wisdom holds that most forms of energy taxes discriminate against lower-income families and individuals. Because these groups spend a higher percentage of their incomes on energy than other income classes do, any tax based on energy—this logic goes—hits these groups disproportionately hard.

One example of the regressive potential of energy taxes is presented in Figure 3. Current energy expenditures on motor fuels and residential energy range from as much as 15 percent for households with incomes below $15,000 to as little as 5 percent of those with incomes above $50,000. Against this backdrop, taxes on energy consumption would appear to fall most heavily on the poor. (As for any differences between different types of energy taxes,

Figure 3. Estimated Energy Expenditures as Percentage of Income

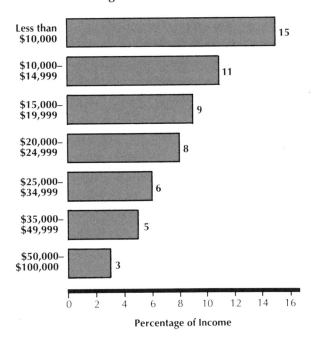

Income	Percentage of Income
Less than $10,000	15
$10,000–$14,999	11
$15,000–$19,999	9
$20,000–$24,999	8
$25,000–$34,999	6
$35,000–$49,999	5
$50,000–$100,000	3

Source: Energy Information Administration, *Studies of Energy Taxes,* U.S. Department of Energy, Washington, D.C. (April 1991)

Table 7 makes it clear that a gasoline tax and a carbon tax have roughly the same distributional characteristics in terms of the tax as a percentage of income.)

Even if energy taxes cannot be called progressive, new research suggests that they may be less burdensome on the poor and middle class than commonly thought.

But there is more to the story than this way of looking at energy taxes suggests. The Congressional Budget Office and other researchers argue that different measures of wealth yield different measures of the burden of a tax.[39] In particular, the Congressional Budget Office and James M. Poterba of the Massachusetts Institute of Technology have shown that if a broader measure of wealth than income—actual expenditures—is used, energy taxes appear less regressive.

(Expenditures represent a more stable long-run measure of wealth than income since they are less related to fluctuations in employment status or earning cycle. They also include government transfer payments, such as Aid to Families with Dependent Children (AFDC), which aren't normally included in income figures.) As Table 8 shows, the impact is more proportional if expenditures are the measure. Even if energy taxes cannot be called progressive, they may be less burdensome on the poor and middle class than commonly thought.

The Impact of Energy Taxes by Region

Energy taxes can redistribute a nation's wealth by region as well as along economic class lines. Because energy production, use, and cost vary by region, some parts of the country will bear a higher tax burden than others. Such potential regional effects can be measured in two ways. First, the tax directly affects energy expenditures by households in the region. The regional tax bill will depend not

Table 7. Estimated Increases in Energy-related Expenditures Resulting from Alternative Energy Taxes

1987 Income	$40 per Ton Carbon Tax	25¢ Gasoline Tax
Average U.S.	242	237
Less than $10,000	173	152
$10,000–$14,999	195	179
$15,000–$19,999	214	206
$20,000–$24,999	237	230
$25,000–$34,999	246	239
$35,000–$49,999	296	298
$50,000 or more	322	318
Below 100% Poverty Line	191	179
Below 125% Poverty Line	195	183

Source: Energy Information Administration. *Studies of Energy Taxes,* U.S. Department of Energy, Washington, D.C., April 1991.

Table 8. Comparison of Estimated Distributional Impacts of a Carbon Tax by Alternative Measures of Income

Distribution Across Income Classes

Income/Expenditure Decile	% of Income	% of Expenditures
1 (Lowest)	10.1	3.7
2	5.0	3.7
3	4.6	3.8
4	4.1	3.7
5	3.6	3.4
6	3.0	3.4
7	2.7	3.2
8	2.3	2.8
9	2.1	2.7
10	1.5	2.3

Source: Poterba, J.M. *Tax Policy to Combat Global Warming: On Designing a Carbon Tax,* Working Paper No. 3649, National Bureau of Economic Research, Inc., March 1991.

only on the tax rate, but also on consumers' ability to adjust their energy use in response to the tax.

The second measure is the indirect (or second-order effects) of the tax on a region's industrial activity, employment, and wealth. As taxes translate into higher energy prices and economic activity adjusts, regions with the most energy-intensive industrial bases may be put at an economic disadvantage relative to other regions. Both of these impacts—the regional expenditure effect and the regional economic effect—deserve policy attention.

■ *Regional Expenditures*—D.E. DeWitt, H. Dowlatabadi, and R.J. Kopp of Resources for the Future have estimated the regional distribution of alternative carbon taxes.[40] As Figure 4 shows, households in certain regions of the country would pay more than others. The difference is most striking between the Pacific northwest states, where cheap subsidized hydropower is readily available, and just about everywhere else.

Differences among other regions are neither great nor insignificant. The average household in New England would pay around 20 percent less in taxes than a household in the north-central states. But, with the exception of the Pacific Northwest, the regions with the highest added tax burdens are also the regions with the lowest existing electricity prices—a function of reliance on low-cost coal as an energy source. Another key variable is households' ability to adjust their purchases in response to the tax and to adopt, for example, more energy-saving products and processes. Regional expenditure estimates rise by almost 15 percent if consumers are assumed to have few options for avoiding the tax. In a "conservation" case, where the Resources for the Future researchers assume that consumers have more

Figure 4. Estimated Changes in Residential Energy Costs from a Carbon Tax by Region

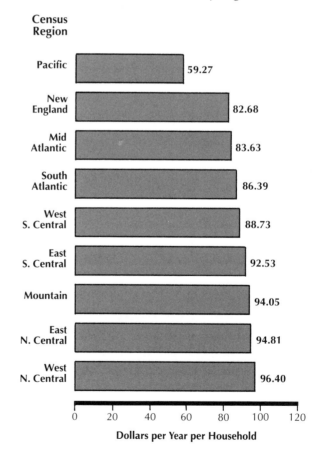

Source: D.E. DeWitt, H. Dowlatabadi, and R.J. Kopp, *Who Bears the Burden of Energy Taxes?,* Resources for the Future, Washington, D.C. (March 1991)

latitude, the absolute impact falls, though the regional difference remains. Unfortunately, this scenario is not very flexible and may not accurately reflect potential economic responses after the tax has been in place for some time.

■ *Regional Economic Impacts*—The relative economic wealth of states or regions can also be affected by carbon tax strategies. States that depend on carbon-based energy sources for generating income or that rely on carbon-based energy-intensive industries could be hurt disproportionately more by a carbon tax on energy than by another form of energy tax. Perhaps predictably, assessing the exact degree to which a state's economy is affected is not a simple matter. In the case of a carbon tax, for example, oil, natural gas, and coal prices would rise, but simply multiplying the amount of the tax by the amount of the fossil fuel resource produced in the state is not a sound measure of economic damage. Instead, the impact of the tax on demand for the fuels and, ultimately, on production levels must be traced.

Virtually all the economic models show that a carbon tax has its greatest impact on coal production. Even the relatively high carbon tax considered by the Congressional Budget Office changes the use of natural gas and oil by only small percentages. *(See Table 9.)* By the same token, all of the reduction in oil demand would come from reducing oil imports.[41] Thus, for the level of taxes considered here, the wealth of oil- and natural gas-producing states would change little. Coal production does decline compared to what it would have been without the tax. Depending on the level of tax, however, much of the reduction in coal demand comes out of anticipated growth in coal use, not reductions in current levels of use.

As shown in Table 9, the Congressional Budget Office has estimated that coal consumption in the short run would fall by approximately 13 percent under a fairly high carbon tax. Consumption of oil and gas falls by significantly lower percentages. A model with a longer-run perspective estimates much higher coal-production impacts with a much lower tax: Jorgenson and Wilcoxen estimate that $17/ton carbon tax will cause coal production to drop by 26 percent. Again, oil and natural gas production falls, but by much smaller amounts. None of the available modeling results show coal production falling below

Table 9. Estimated Effects of a Carbon Charge of $100 per Ton on Prices and Use of Fossil Fuels in the United States in 2000

(Percentage changes from baseline levels)

	Oil	Natural Gas	Coal	All Energy
Prices	21	16	161	n.a.
Use	– 3	– 4	– 13	– 7

Source: Congress of the United States, Congressional Budget Office. *Carbon Charges as a Response to Global Warming: The Effects of Taxing Fossil Fuels,* U.S. Government Printing Office, Washington, D.C., August 1990.

current production levels—at least for the levels of taxes considered in this paper. CO_2-reduction commitments beyond stabilization or 20-percent reductions are likely to require much deeper reductions in coal production.

No published modeling results disaggregate energy tax burdens on specific industries at the state or regional level. It is not possible, therefore, to specify the degree to which the GNP effects of carbon taxes would be borne by any specific state or how coal production in Wyoming is reduced relative to that in West Virginia. The states at first-order risk, however, are relatively easy to identify. As Figure 5 shows, three states—Wyoming, Kentucky and West Virginia—account for over half of total U.S. coal production. No doubt, they would bear a significant fraction of the costs of lost production.

The Impact of Carbon Taxes by Industry

Not surprisingly, carbon taxes would fall most heavily and directly on the energy-production sectors—coal mining in particular—and on industries that depend on coal. As the initial price increases are passed on to final consumers (or back to shareholders), however, the economic burdens of the tax would spread to other industries and sectors. As

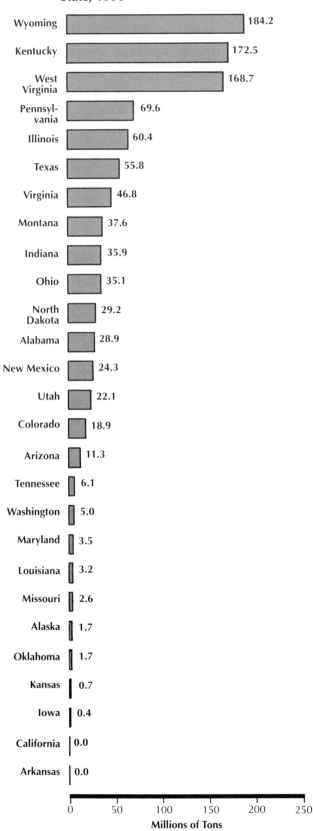

Figure 5. United States Coal Production by State, 1990

State	Millions of Tons
Wyoming	184.2
Kentucky	172.5
West Virginia	168.7
Pennsylvania	69.6
Illinois	60.4
Texas	55.8
Virginia	46.8
Montana	37.6
Indiana	35.9
Ohio	35.1
North Dakota	29.2
Alabama	28.9
New Mexico	24.3
Utah	22.1
Colorado	18.9
Arizona	11.3
Tennessee	6.1
Washington	5.0
Maryland	3.5
Louisiana	3.2
Missouri	2.6
Alaska	1.7
Oklahoma	1.7
Kansas	0.7
Iowa	0.4
California	0.0
Arkansas	0.0

Source: Energy Information Administration, *Coal Production 1990*, EIA-0118(90), U.S. Department of Energy, Washington, D.C. (1991)

Figure 6 demonstrates, a carbon tax is likely to have broadly distributed industrial impacts. In this regard, a carbon tax resembles other broad-based energy taxes, all of which tend to raise energy prices and thus hurt heavy energy users. The ultimate impact on the performance of any individual industry is a function of how well that industry embraces energy efficiency, switches to fuels that are taxed less, or passes on the price increase to consumers or back to coal-production sources.

The primary metals, chemicals, and petroleum-refining industries are the other three carbon-intensive industries in the U.S. economy. Of these, the domestic petroleum-refining industry would be the most likely to suffer from reduced demand for its product. In the other carbon-intensive industries, the tax bill for a $40 per ton carbon tax would not exceed 2 percent of the value of shipments of manufactured products.[42] If any efficiency- or fuel-switching measures are taken, the tax bill could be substantially less. Some industries, of course, would benefit from the tax. These might include, for instance, plastics recyclers, biomass producers (including both the agricultural and processing components), and solar power industries. It is difficult to predict where these industries might locate, but they are likely to be more geographically dispersed than existing energy industries.

If the net economic gains associated with revenues from a carbon tax are recycled back into the economy, more industries will win than lose.

It is extremely important to note that the net economic gains associated with recycling the revenues from a carbon tax back into the economy suggest that more industries will win than lose. Everything being equal, lower corporate capital or labor tax rates would benefit many industries particularly those in which energy is a small element of their overall production costs. Communication and information services, financial services, medicine and

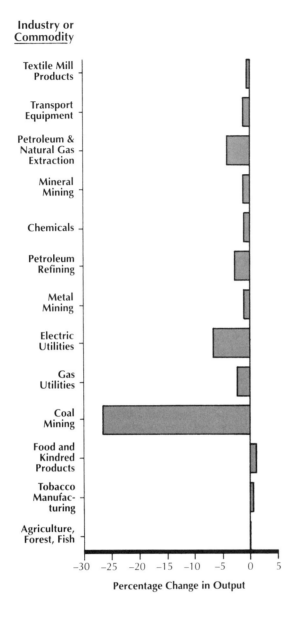

Figure 6. Effect on Industrial Sectors of a Carbon Tax

Industry or
Commodity

Textile Mill Products
Transport Equipment
Petroleum & Natural Gas Extraction
Mineral Mining
Chemicals
Petroleum Refining
Metal Mining
Electric Utilities
Gas Utilities
Coal Mining
Food and Kindred Products
Tobacco Manufacturing
Agriculture, Forest, Fish

−30 −25 −20 −15 −10 −5 0 5

Percentage Change in Output

Source: D.W. Jorgenson and P.J. Wilcoxen, "Reducing U.S. Carbon Dioxide Emissions: The Cost of Different Goals," in J. Moroney (ed.), <u>Energy Growth and the Environment</u>, Vol. 7, JAI Press, Greenwich, Connecticut (1992)

tax with lower tax rates for other impacts to production.

How to Address the Distributional Impacts

Of the three major distributional impacts identified earlier, the differential impact on carbon-intensive industries can be partially offset by lowering capital or labor costs economy-wide through lower capital and payroll tax rates. Reducing marginal income tax rates for lower-income people would address some of the price impacts on these households. In contrast, the price impact on very low-income households and the impact on coal-producing regions require more specific compensation efforts.

Addressing Low Income Groups

Many forms of federal and state taxation are regressive, and most consumption taxes hurt lower- and middle-income groups more than the wealthy. But because energy taxes have not been widely used in this country (with the exception of federal and state gas taxes), it is not surprising that designing programs to offset their regressive nature poses both a technical and a political challenge. (Some programs were initiated during the 1970s in response to the energy price spikes of that decade, but many of these have been cut back or abandoned as real energy prices have subsequently fallen.)

To help policy-makers consider this challenge, the Congressional Budget Office and the Center for Budget and Policy Priorities have prepared similar analyses of alternative means for addressing tax regressivity.[43] While these reports don't specifically focus on carbon or energy taxes, they do provide a blueprint for compensating taxpayers for regressive taxes in general. These analyses suggest a compensation program that contains four major elements.[44]

■ *Expand the Earned Income Tax Credit*—The Earned Income Tax Credit (EITC) is a refundable tax credit. Its virtue is that it applies to low-income working families with children—an important subset of low-income groups hit by an energy tax. On the other hand, it does not address the needs of non-working families or families without children, and an income tax return has to be filed to get the credit.

■ *Increase Food Stamp Benefits*—Food stamp benefits are available basically to all households with

other high technology industries are likely to grow faster under tax reform initiatives of this sort. Certainly industries that offer low or no carbon energy services would also gain under a carbon tax coupled with a tax shift. On a national level, aggregate productivity and growth would rise. None of the distributional estimates presented here portray these beneficial economic effects of combining a carbon income and assets below a certain level. An increase in these benefits would reach qualifying households ineligible for EITC. (For perspective here, the food stamp program has a low participation rate.)

■ *Increase the Standard Deduction*—An energy tax hits middle-income households disproportionately, as well as the low-income households covered by the first two programs. Increasing the size of the standard deduction available to federal income tax filers would directly benefit moderate-income households. For example, one study estimates that a $500-increase in the standard deduction would return $75 to the average taxpayer (who does not itemize deductions) and would cost around $3 billion.[45] Seventy-five dollars is roughly two thirds of the additional energy expenditures incurred by households with incomes between $20,000 and $25,000.

■ *Increase the Supplemental Security Income (SSI) Program*—The three programs listed above miss, in large part, low-income elderly households and disabled individuals. Because these groups' program benefits are usually tied to inflation, it is sometimes argued that they are less affected by excise tax increases that ultimately show up in higher consumer prices. But energy tax increases may be underrepresented in the consumer price index and, as such, not fully compensated by cost-of-living adjustments. To the extent that this is true, an increase in SSI benefits, a major form of income for households headed by the elderly or disabled, could compensate these groups for higher energy taxes or expenditures.

Two other existing federal programs could also be used to directly reduce the tax burden on low- and moderate-income consumers. The first and most important is the federal Low Income Weatherization Assistance Program (WAP). WAP provides an average of up to $1600 in home energy-efficiency improvements—attic and wall insulation, upgraded and new furnaces, etc. Unfortunately, the program is not fully funded, and only about one fourth of the 12 to 17 million eligible households have received services to date.[46] Expanding this program would reduce energy bills and, therefore, carbon tax bills for low-income households and would give these households a direct and affordable means of reducing carbon emissions.

The Low Income Energy Assistance Program (LEAP) is the second existing program that could be used to help low- and moderate-income people adjust to fuel-price increases. It has the advantage of reaching low-income consumers quickly, but it may not encourage emissions reductions (and may actually encourage the release of more emissions by reducing the marginal cost of home heating energy), and it doesn't generate returns on investment greater than 1 to 1.

This brief discussion points to some possible programs to offset regressivity. But it also makes it clear that no one program is likely to address all affected groups. In designing an offset package, the preference should be to use reductions in other tax rates. Properly crafted, these could provide tax-reform benefits, as well as cope with some of the distributional impacts. Obviously, special programs may be required to help individuals who are outside the current federal tax system.

Coping with Coal-Producing States

Table 10 identifies the states that will bear the brunt of the coal-production losses. A state's burden from a carbon tax is the sum of the losses accruing to four major groups:

■ state taxpayers whose tax base shrinks (as a result of reductions in revenues from severance taxes, for example);

■ owners of coal resources whose real wealth declines;

■ coal miners who lose their jobs; and

■ firms and industries that support coal-mining operations and workers (shops, stores, etc.).

The actual dollar loss associated with these categories is difficult to estimate; it depends, in part, on what would happen in the absence of a carbon tax. For perspective, coal-mining employment levels have been falling even though coal production has risen. Increased production of western coal (which is capital-intensive) and increased mechanization of eastern coal mines have already led to losses in the mining population, and many Appalachian coal regions are already amid an economic transition. Between 1980 and 1989, for example, coal employment fell by 43 percent to a total of 116,000 workers (in 1989), while coal production increased by approximately 30 percent. Under moderate tax schemes, coal-production falls relative to what it would have been but still grows in absolute terms (although this may vary from state to state).

Calculations of economic losses due to a carbon tax should take coal types into account too. Most carbon tax proposals assume implicitly that all types of coal contain the same amount of carbon, but they don't. Eastern bituminous coals can contain as little as 40 percent carbon or as much as 80 percent. Western sub-bituminous coal typically has lower percentages and less variation. A carbon tax based on an average carbon content will push coal users, everything else being equal, to pick coals with higher carbon contents (and generally higher energy values) than average since the price per unit of carbon is the same.

These mitigating factors aside, carbon taxes as a whole do fall most heavily on coal production, and coal-producing states or sectors are likely to demand fair compensation for their losses. Even though other states or regions have undergone comparably great economic transitions over the last 100 years, fairness dictates that these states receive some aid to ease the costs of a transition triggered entirely by environmental policy.

Carbon taxes as a whole fall most heavily on coal production, and coal-producing states or sectors are likely to demand fair compensation for their losses.

Federal or state spending or tax programs could be designed to offset the burdens of a carbon tax borne by specific states. Enterprise zones, job training and relocation programs, or early retirement programs are obvious examples. But since the needs of affected states will vary greatly, no single set of policies will work in all coal-producing regions. Rather, a block-grant program might be more appropriate, giving states the flexibility to design their own programs.[47] One basis for determining grant size might be state-specific estimates of coal-production losses. Alternatively, a pool for revenue sharing could be politically determined and then allocated on the basis of each state's share of total production. As an illustration of this approach, Table 10 allocates a hypothetical block grant trust fund of $1.8 billion among

the coal-producing states. (Allocations range from $100,000 for Arkansas to $337.6 million for Wyoming.) This compensation strategy lets states develop programs that address their special circumstances, regardless of the size of the trust fund. It does have one serious draw-back, however. To ensure that the funds will be available continually to states, it may be necessary to create a trust fund that is not subject to annual appropriations even though such funds are generally not politically popular, except to the beneficiaries.

International Trade and Competitiveness

A carbon tax imposed in the United States alone would raise the cost of carbon-dependent domestic products in the short run relative to international competitors, even though energy prices in Europe and Japan, for example, are already much higher than U.S. prices. The net effect, some argue, would be an increased trade deficit, lost competitiveness, and perhaps relocation of U.S. manufacturing abroad.

The precise impact on the U.S. trade balance of this rise in energy prices is difficult to identify and may shift over time. But impacts are likely to be minor. Since total energy costs comprise less than 4 percent of the costs of manufacturing for all goods and services, the effect of a moderate carbon tax is likely to be lost in the noise of international exchange rates and other factors influencing the relative costs of U.S. goods. A $40 per ton carbon tax would amount to less than 1 percent, on average, of U.S. manufacturing value of shipments and would decline thereafter. In the four most energy-intensive industries, the tax would amount to around 2 percent of the value of shipments. If the beneficial effects to these firms of lowering other tax rates or lowered capital and labor costs are considered, total production costs for many industries could *fall*. Further, energy costs are only one of many variables that affect industrial location decisions, and attempts to test how environmental control costs affect location choices have never demonstrated a positive relationship.

A further balance-of-trade advantage is that a carbon tax lowers U.S. demand for oil. Most of the models reviewed here show that with a carbon tax, oil imports would fall, not use of domestic oil. To the extent that this is true, the U.S. balance of trade

Table 10. Hypothetical Trust Fund for Coal Producing States

State	Coal Produced (million short tons)	% of Total Coal Produced	Allocations ($ million)
Wyoming	171.6	19	337.6
Kentucky	166.5	18	327.6
West Virginia	153.1	17	301.4
Pennsylvania	73.8	8	136.9
Illinois	50.3	6	98.9
Virginia	42.8	5	84.2
Montana	37.7	4	74.3
Indiana	33.6	4	66.2
Ohio	33.6	4	66.0
North Dakota	29.6	3	58.2
Alabama	27.9	3	54.9
New Mexico	23.7	3	46.6
Utah	20.1	2	39.6
Colorado	17.1	2	33.6
Arizona	11.9	1	23.4
Tennessee	6.4	1	12.5
Washington	5.0	1	9.9
Missouri	3.4	0	6.7
Maryland	3.3	0	6.6
Louisiana	2.9	0	5.9
Oklahoma	1.7	0	3.4
Alaska	1.6	0	3.2
Kansas	0.9	0	1.7
Iowa	0.4	0	0.8
California	0.0	0	0.1
Arkansas	0.0	0	0.1
TOTAL	914.7	100.00	1800.0

Source: World Resources Institute

will improve. In addition, reductions in imports could reduce world oil prices. For example, the Energy Information Administration estimates that with a $40 carbon tax, lower world oil prices (as a result of lower U.S. demand for oil) would further reduce the oil-import bill over the next decade by nearly $19 billion.[48] This trade advantage is nearly five times larger than the domestic welfare loss that EIA estimates the taxes will cause.

The ultimate impact of an environmental tax on the domestic trade balance would depend, in the case of a carbon tax, on whether the tax was used to finance the lower capital and labor tax rates, the degree to which oil imports are lowered, and what mix of outputs emerges as the domestic economy responds to higher energy prices. Presumably, the overall effect would be small or nonexistent. Indeed, studies of U.S. competitiveness—such as MIT's recent

Made in America—rarely mention energy prices as a significant concern.[49] Nevertheless, the impact on carbon-intensive goods that are traded could be more significant. As a result, it may be important from a trade perspective to consider federal policies (tax or otherwise) that would help minimize any detrimental trade effects.

The ultimate impact of a carbon tax on the domestic trade balance would depend on whether the tax was used to finance the lower capital and labor tax rates, the degree to which oil imports are lowered, and what mix of outputs emerges as the domestic economy responds to higher energy prices.

Including impacts of carbon-bearing goods in the tax scheme would be the most straightforward approach to reducing the trade impact on carbon-intensive products. While imports of raw carbon-bearing fuels would be taxed under most carbon tax programs, products containing carbon or produced using fossil fuels from outside the United States would not be subject to the tax. Including imports of these goods would equalize the relative price advantage of imports not subject to a domestic carbon tax. Measuring and monitoring the direct and implicit carbon content of imports would be difficult, but probably not impossible, at least in terms of first-order quantities. The U.S. tax on CFCs is applied to imports of a wide range of consumer and industrial goods.[50]

Rather than taxing imports, it can be tempting to reduce the trade impacts of a carbon tax by either broadening or restricting the basis of the tax. The European Commission energy/carbon tax proposal *(see Box 4)* has, in fact, done both. It combines a broad-based energy tax and a carbon tax: the burden on the European export markets, many of which are fossil-fuel based, is reduced by including non-carbon sources of energy (in particular, nuclear energy in

France) and excluding certain petrochemical and energy-intensive industries.

A major rationale for changing the basis of a carbon tax is to change the distribution of the economic impacts—certainly the prime motivation behind the different kinds of carbon taxes used in Europe. Changing the universe of carbon sources to which the tax applies may reduce the burden of the tax on specific sectors, though it also penalizes those who make cost-effective carbon dioxide reductions. In general, however, it might be cheaper to shift the burden of the tax in the other ways discussed below.

One set of tax exemptions may be consistent with CO_2 emission-reduction goals. Some carbon-based fuels are not burned but are instead turned into long-lasting products (such as plastics) that sequester or hold carbon for decades. This form of fossil fuel consumption entails no carbon-dioxide emissions—at least not within a policy-relevant time period. Exempting these uses of fossil fuels from a carbon tax through a tax credit, for example, could give industries that are inoffensive from a carbon standpoint a break without affecting emission reductions.[51] Just as important, exempting sequestered carbon products would reduce the trade impacts of a carbon tax, particularly since many of these products are high-value exports subject to strong international competition. The environmental case for a feedstock exemption is, however, not clear cut. Many products developed from petrochemical feedstocks may be returned to the atmosphere quite quickly—fertilizers, pesticides, and plastics that are incinerated as trash are a few examples. Further, the amount of carbon involved is quite small, suggesting that any economic or trade effect from exempting feedstocks is also likely to be small.

In the longer run, the competitiveness of the United States relative to that of our major trading partners will be determined by our ability to improve and sustain the productivity of our workforce. Meeting this goal requires an adequate stream of capital investments. Coupling a carbon tax with broader tax-reform initiatives could create such incentives. Just as important, some industries are likely to benefit directly from a carbon-reduction strategy. Producers of renewable-energy and energy-efficiency technologies comprise just one set of potential winners. Much of this equipment is traded internationally.

Developing these industries domestically would spur opportunities abroad, especially as other nations pursue energy-efficiency and renewable-energy alternatives.

BOX 4. THE EUROPEAN EXPERIENCE WITH CARBON TAXES

European nations have a longer history than the United States does of using energy taxes as revenue sources and a means of discouraging certain energy-consuming activities. Not surprisingly, therefore, Europeans became interested in carbon taxes early. Several countries have recently enacted or proposed carbon taxes as a means of meeting stated CO_2-reduction goals. Further, the European Commission has proposed an energy/carbon tax for its member countries.

While conventional wisdom holds that Europe taxes energy higher than the United States, this is true only for some forms of energy consumption and for some countries. Gasoline and other oil products are taxed quite heavily throughout Europe, but coal production is often subsidized rather than taxed.[52] Natural gas is typically taxed, if at all, at much lower levels than oil. As Table 11 shows, high taxes on gasoline translate into fairly significant carbon taxes, and few industrialized countries tax other forms of energy significantly.

Country-Specific Carbon Tax Programs

Several examples of European carbon tax proposals are presented in Table 12. Most of them follow a similar design. Through numerous exceptions and rate differentials, the taxes protect certain sectors that would otherwise bear the principal burden of a true carbon tax. These taxes do not necessarily lead to cost-effective carbon reductions. In fact, many of these taxes are so small that they are unlikely to lead to any CO_2 reduction at all.

Many European carbon tax proposals call for reductions in other energy taxes. This is part of a larger trend in Europe to substitute pollution or "green" taxes for other tax programs. Part of this trend is reflected in the shifting of a portion of existing energy taxes into carbon-based taxes. The tax offset is not necessarily aimed at producing revenue neutrality, but is often an acknowledgment that some energy tax rates are already quite high. For example, in January, 1991 Sweden introduced a carbon tax that applies to fossil fuels used in the domestic sector,

Table 11. Implicit Carbon Taxes in 1988
($ per ton of carbon)

	Oil and Oil Products	Gas	Coal	Total
United States	65	0	0	28
Japan	130	2	0	79
Germany	212	23	0	95
France	351	38	0	229
Italy	317	80	0	223
United Kingdom	297	0	0	106
Canada	108	0	0	52
Austria	267	39	0	150
Belgium	162	35	0	86
Denmark	297	110	0	147
Finland	189	0	0	107
Ireland	277	4	0	138
Netherlands	221	27	0	89
New Zealand	235	0	0	117
Norway	258	0	0	182
Portugal	205	131	0	150
Spain	176	19	0	112
Sweden	268	13	6	214
Switzerland	224	2	18	198

Source: Hoeller, P. and M. Wallin. *Energy Prices, Taxes and Carbon Dioxide Emission*, Economics and Statistics Department Working Papers, No. 106, Organisation for Economic Co-Operation and Development, Paris, 1991.

industry that is not energy-intensive, cars, and domestic air traffic. When the tax was introduced, some gasoline taxes were reduced so that there was no net increase in the tax on gasoline. Table 13 highlights the key elements of the Swedish carbon tax proposal and the related energy-tax reforms.

Box 4 continues

Table 12. International Carbon Taxes

Country	Fuel	Tax	Enacted
Norway	gasoline	10¢/litre	
	fuel oil	5¢/litre	
Finland	light and heavy heating and fuel oil	2–3%	November 1991
	peat	5%	
	natural gas	2%	
	coal	8% ($5.64/ton)	
	total	$61 million in 1991	
Netherlands	fossil fuels	$2/ton carbon	February 1990
Sweden	all CO_2 emissions	4¢/kg	January 1991
	coal	$105.40/ton	
	natural gas	$90.95/m³	
	cars	7¢/litre LPG	
	other	$127.50/ton of LPG	
	gasoline	10¢/litre	
	CO_2 emissions on domestic air traffic	13¢/ton of fuel	
Denmark	electricity consumption from coal and oil-fired plants	$14.28/ton CO_2 $52/ton carbon	Fall 1991

Source: World Resources Institute

The European Community Carbon Tax Proposal

The European Commission, the European Community's (EC) executive body, proposed a combination energy/carbon tax to its 12 member nations in a September 1991 "communication" outlining the community's strategy to limit carbon dioxide and improve energy efficiency. That tax proposal has since evolved into a draft of an official EC directive, the Community's equivalent to national legislation. Under the commission proposal, the energy component of the tax would be levied on all fossil and nuclear energy to promote efficiency regardless of its source. However, all renewable sources of energy—except large-scale hydroelectric schemes—would be exempt so as to promote alternative energy production. The carbon component of the tax would account for the amount of carbon dioxide emitted when a fuel is burnt. The proposal calls for a tax of $3 a barrel of oil or its equivalent to be introduced in 1993. This amount would increase annually by $1 until it reaches $10 a barrel in 2000. Assuming a tax scheme based half on most of the energy used and half on the carbon content of the energy used, the fully phased-in equivalent taxes for coal and nuclear power would be $14 and $5, respectively. The Commission estimates that in 2000 the tax would increase industrial coal prices by 58 percent, while prices for the oil and natural gas used for industrial purposes would rise 45 percent and 34 percent. The price of gasoline would rise 6 percent by 2000, and diesel would increase 11 percent.[53] (Such figures, however, must be considered tentative since disagreement

Table 13. Fuel Price Implications of the Swedish Tax Reform (US$)

EFFECT OF TAX REFORM ON EXCISE TAXES
(Jan. 1991)

	Energy Tax	CO$_2$ Tax	Sulphur Tax	Total Tax	Change Against December 1990
Gasoline (1,000 litre)	448.80	98.60	••	547.40	0
Diesel Oil (1,000 litre)	91.80	122.40	••	214.20	+ 54.40
Light Fuel Oil for Industry (1,000 litre)	91.80	122.40	9.18	223.38	+ 40.12
Light Fuel Oil for Households (1,000 litre)	91.80	122.40	9.18	223.38	0
Heavy Fuel Oil for Industry (metric tons)	91.80	122.40	36.72	250.92	+ 67.66
Natural Gas for Households (1,000m³)	29.75	90.95	••	120.70	+ 61.20
Steam Coal Price, Industry (metric ton)	39.10	105.40	38.25	182.75	+ 104.55

Source: Hoeller, P. and M. Wallin. *Energy Prices, Taxes and Carbon Dioxide Emission,* Economics and Statistics Department Working Papers, No. 106, Organisation for Economic Co-Operation and Development, Paris, 1991.

•• not applicable

remains about what percentage of the tax would be based on energy use versus the carbon content of the fuel.)

In crafting the proposal, the Commission attempted to reduce some of the more explicit burdens associated with a pure carbon tax. First, the 50/50 split on energy and carbon content takes some of the onus off the coal industry and coal users. Second, the commission included provisions to protect consumers and specific energy-intensive industries.

■ The proposal emphasizes that the tax should be revenue-neutral from the taxpayer's standpoint.

The Commission encourages each country to offset the energy/carbon tax by decreasing other tax burdens on individuals and companies. The estimated revenue of ECU 50 billion (US$65 billion) would be collected and used by the individual governments, so responsibility for implementing the principle of revenue neutrality lies with each nation.

■ In order to "maintain the competitiveness of the Community" in world markets, energy-intensive industrial sectors (defined as those industries where energy costs exceed 8 percent of total production costs) are provided a graduated tax reduction or refund. For example, firms with energy costs that exceed 30 percent of total production costs have their tax burden reduced by 90 percent. In addition, individual firms may be exempted completely from paying the tax, provided that they have undertaken substantial energy-savings or carbon dioxide reduction measures.

■ Most importantly, the current draft of the directive makes the application of the tax conditional on the introduction of a "similar tax or of measures that have an equivalent financial impact" by other members of the Organisation for Economic Co-operation and Development (OECD). Though some argue that this provision will effectively kill the directive, many in the EC view the conditionality clause as a valuable mechanism to encourage international debate about the carbon tax, particularly in Japan and the United States.

The draft directive, now being debated by various ministerial groups, remains somewhat vague. But it does contain some analyses. According to the proposal, only modest macroeconomic costs will result as long as a revenue-neutral tax is introduced gradually and predictably. The EC as a whole would experience some reduction in the annual economic growth rate (between .05 and .1 percentage points) and a temporary increase in the rate of inflation (.3 to .5 per annum). Any positive effects that might result from the policy are not cited in the proposal.

The EC tax proposal is far from becoming law. The Commission's communication to the members of the EC and the resulting draft directive are meant to elicit open dialogue among representatives from each state, thereby moving the Community toward consensus. Further work by the Commission and various ministerial groups will undoubtedly result in revisions to the directive as it now stands. Formal action to accept the tax hinges on many contentious issues, the most controversial being conditionality. Regardless if this new obstacle can be removed, close scrutiny can be expected since, under the rules of the Single European Act, all taxation issues require a unanimous decision.[54]

* * *

Efforts by national governments to reduce emissions of CO_2 do not have to burden domestic economies. In fact, they can have the opposite effect. But the outcome does depend on how governments choose to do it. A carbon tax strategy that recycles the revenues from a carbon tax and links them to economically productive tax reform will create new economic opportunities that can actually improve overall welfare. Other approaches are unlikely to provide similar opportunities. Of course, even if the economy can be made more robust as a whole, some groups will be worse off, as a result of the new tax. But it is not necessary to forego all of the economic advantages of a tax-based approach to carbon reductions to protect the disadvantaged. Carefully targeted compensation programs can redress distributional inequities and leave the economic benefits intact.

If a carbon tax strategy has all of these valuable attributes, why isn't it the program of choice in the United States? The answer to this question lies in the politics of taxation in the United States and a fundamental public distrust of government's willingness to raise one tax and lower another. But even though both these obstacles are ingrained and formidable, the economic and environmental benefits of a carbon tax strategy would reward the nation handsomely for overcoming political inertia and suspicion.

Roger C. Dower is currently Director of the Climate, Energy and Pollution Program at the World Resources Institute. Prior to coming to WRI, he was Chief of the Energy and Environment Unit at the Congressional Budget Office, U.S. Congress. Before that, he was Research Director at the Environmental Law Institute. **Mary Beth Zimmerman** is a Project Manager at the Alliance to Save Energy. Prior to joining the Alliance in 1988, Ms. Zimmerman served as Senior Staff Associate at the National Governors' Association, Committee on Energy and Environment. Ms. Zimmerman served also as a Research Assistant at Resources for the Future, Energy and Minerals Division.

NOTES

1. There are several recent discussions of this point. *See* in particular; Congress of the United States, Congressional Budget Office. *Carbon Charges as a Response to Global Warming: The Effects of Taxing Fossil Fuels* (Washington, DC: U.S. Government Printing Office, August 1990), and Dornbusch, Rudiger and James M. Poterba (editors). *Global Warming: Economic Policy Responses,* (Cambridge: The MIT Press, 1991).

2. Although the nature and extent of the impacts may differ.

3. A useful summary of the science of climate change and its potential risks can be found in: *Climate Change: The IPCC Scientific Assessment,* Intergovernmental Panel on Climate Change, J. T. Houghton, G.J. Jenkins and J.J. Ephraums (eds.), Cambridge, 1990.

4. *See* Energy Information Administration, NES Service Report #2 (SR.NES/90-02), "Energy Consumption and Conservation Potential: Supporting Analysis for the NES," December 21, 1990.

5. "The Changing Atmosphere: Implications for Global Security," statement from international meeting sponsored by the Government of Canada in Toronto, June 27–30, 1988.

6. Worldwide, carbon contributes 66 percent of total greenhouse gas emissions (weighted by extent of contribution to total warming), a number which is expected to increase over time. Carbon emissions constitute 53 percent of total U.S. emissions.

7. Another more direct means is a system of emission permits, as described in this report.

8. Several recent studies have suggested or investigated variations of this basic carbon tax. These include a sales tax weighted by carbon content, a unit carbon tax weighted by the end-use elasticity and a simple fossil fuel tax. Each of these options raise the long-run cost per ton of carbon reduced relative to a carbon tax, and shift some of the burden of the tax away from coal.

9. Emissions of SO_2 and NO_x are controlled under the 1990 Clean Air Act Amendments. If the level of control is already "optimal"—that is, if the value of the last ton of SO_2 and NO_x emissions reduced is precisely equal to the cost of reducing it—then no further reductions would be justified under a traditional cost-benefit framework. This does not imply that additional reductions would have no environmental benefit, only that the benefit alone would not justify the cost of additional reductions. In this case, however, the benefits are a windfall of climate policy and should therefore be counted among the benefits of promoting climate stability.

10. One set of regulatory policies for CO_2 emission reductions are quite different from regulatory control programs. Regulatory changes can sometimes overcome or compensate for market failures. Changes in the way electric and gas utilities are regulated, for instance, can allow energy efficiency improvements and renewable (non-carbon) energy sources to compete on a more equal basis with traditional fossil fuels. These kinds of market reforms improve market performance, and may also improve the effectiveness of any pollution tax or permit system.

11. Bradley, et al., evaluate a greenhouse gas tax which includes methane and other greenhouse gas emissions along with carbon. They also evaluate a carbon tax with reforestation credits.

12. Tietenberg provides a very useful review and discussion of the dollar cost savings that might be associated with various economic incentive type pollution control programs. *See*: Tietenberg, T.H., *Emissions Trading: An Exercise in Reforming Pollution Policy,* Resources for the Future, Washington, D.C., 1985.

13. Some of these points are treated more fully in Parker, Larry, *Coal Market Effects of CO_2 Control Strategies as Embodied in H.R. 1086 and H.R. 2663,* Congressional Research Service, 91-883ENR, 1991.

14. *See:* Oates, W.E. and P.R. Portney, "Economic Incentives for Controlling Greenhouse Gases," *Resources,* Spring 1991.

15. There is an inverse relationship between the revenues raised by a carbon tax and the environmental benefits. As consumers and producers lower their use of carbon bearing fuels and products in response to the tax, revenues fall, but the environment improves. In theory, a tax set high enough would not generate any revenues. In practice, however, this is highly unlikely. As the economic models reviewed later show, there will generally always be some level of emission reduction that costs more than paying the tax. Even at fairly high tax rates, CO_2 is still emitted and revenues collected. All of the revenue estimates and economic impacts discussed in this report take into account the behavioral responses to the tax and can be thought of as net revenues in the sense that they already take account of tax-avoidance behavior.

16. Of course, the provision of public services such as schools or roads can provide more than a dollar's worth of benefit, and public expenditures can have a large impact on productivity. The discussion in this report is limited to the overall impact on productivity and output of different strategies for raising the funds for these expenditures.

17. This is based on estimates provided in Jorgenson, Dale W. and Kun-Young Yun. "The Excess Burden of Taxation in the U.S.," HIER Discussion Paper No. 1528 (Cambridge: Harvard University, November 1990) which calculated an average efficiency cost of the entire tax system to be 18 percent.

18. The federal and state revenue estimates for 1990 were derived from U.S. Government, *Economic Report of the President* (Washington, DC: U.S. Government Printing Office, February 1991), Tables B-81 and B-82.

19. The range is based on the average and marginal cost estimates for capital taxes presented in Table 4.

20. In a recent study of carbon taxes, the author states, "The relevance of these findings (in reference to the economic benefits of tax reform with carbon taxes), however, could be questioned. Forging a link between an increase in one tax and a decrease in another tax is a matter of politics rather than economics." David W. Montgomery, *The Costs of Controlling Carbon Dioxide Emissions,* Charles River Associates, December 1991.

21. This point has been made before and is developed more fully in, Oates, W.E., "Pollution Charges as a Source of Public Revenues," Discussion Paper QE92-05, Resources for the Future, Washington, D.C., 1991.

22. *See* in particular, Nordhaus, W.D., "Economic approaches to Greenhouse Warming," in *Global Warming: Economic Policy Responses,* Dornbusch, R. and J.M. Poterba (eds.), MIT Press, 1991.

23. Cline, William R., *Global Warming: The Economic Stakes,* Institute for International Economics, Washington, D.C., 1992.

24. Technically, the models actually measure something called "consumer welfare," although the models only consider the impact of goods and services included in GNP as a part of that welfare.

25. For a careful review of the adjustment costs of energy price changes, see: Bohi, D.R., *Energy Price Shocks and Macroeconomic Performance,* Resources for the Future, Washington, D.C., 1989.

26. Technically, the revenues do not disappear. The underlying assumption is that they are returned on a lump-sum basis without affecting marginal tax rates or the deficit.

27. Energy Information Administration, *Studies on Energy Taxes,* SR/EMEU/91-02, U.S. Department of Energy, April, 1991.

28. Bradley, Richard A., Edward C. Watts, Edward Williams, "Limiting Net Greenhouse Gas Emissions in the United States," Vol. II, pg. 9.9, U.S. DOE, September, 1991.

29. OTA, *Changing by Degrees: Steps to Reduce Greenhouse Gases,* Congress of the United States, OTA-0-482, February 1991; ICF Incorporated, *Preliminary Technology Cost Estimates of Measures Available to Reduce U.S. Greenhouse Gas Emissions by 2010,* submitted to U.S. E.P.A., August 1990; National Academy of Sciences, *Policy Implications of Greenhouse Warming,* National Academy Press, Washington, D.C., 1991.

30. When Alan Manne and Richard Richels allow energy-efficiency improvements of 1 percent per annum, the cumulative cost of emissions reductions

over 100 years falls from $3.6 to $1.8 trillion dollars. "$CO_2$ Emission Limits: An Economic Cost Analysis for the USA," *The Energy Journal,* Vol. 11, No. 2, pp. 51–74, April 1990.

31. Hogan, "Input Management and Oil Emergencies," in Deise, D. and Joseph Nye (eds.) *Energy Security,* Cambridge, MA: Ballinger, 1981.

32. Manne, Alan S. and Richard G. Richels, "CO_2 Emission Limits: An Economic Cost Analysis for the USA," *The Energy Journal,* April 1990.

33. Jorgenson, Dale W. and Peter J. Wilcoxen, "Energy Prices and U.S. Economic Growth," prepared for the Panel on Policy Implications of Global Warming, Committee on Science, Engineering, and Public Policy, March 14, 1990.

34. Energy Information Administration, *Studies on Energy Taxes,* SR/EMEU/91-02, U.S. Department of Energy, April, 1991.

35. U.S. Department of Energy, *Limiting Net Greenhouse Gas Emissions in the United States,* Washington, D.C., 1991.

36. Experience with tree planting for carbon sequestration is limited and researchers are only beginning to develop a firm sense of the marginal costs of these programs. It is not clear whether the low costs presented in most existing studies will actually hold over large programs. For a more extensive discussion of these issues see, Trexler, M., *Minding the Carbon Store,* World Resources Institute, 1991.

37. U.S. Department of Energy, *Limiting Net Greenhouse Emissions in the United States,* Executive Summary, Washington, D.C., 1990, p. 7.

38. There are, however, many other different notions and definitions of fairness. The "polluter pays principle," intergenerational equity, and the beneficiary pays principle all embody concepts of fairness that would lead to different views concerning the distributional effects of carbon taxes.

39. Congress of the United States, Congressional Budget Office. *Federal Taxation of Tobacco, Alcoholic Beverages, and Motor Fuels* (Washington, DC: U.S. Government Printing Office, August 1990), and Poterba, J.M. "Tax Policy to Combat Global Warming: On Designing a Carbon Tax," in Dornbusch, Rudiger and James M. Poterba (Editors). *Global Warming: Economic Policy Responses* (Cambridge: The MIT Press, 1991).

40. DeWitt, D.E., H. Dowlatabadi and R.J. Kopp, *Who Bears the Burden of Energy Taxes,* Discussion Paper QE91-12, Washington, D.C.

41. Congressional Budget Office, *Carbon Charges as a Response to Global Warming: the Effects of Taxing Fossil Fuels,* August, 1990, p. 32.

42. Calculations based on EIA, "Manufacturing Energy Consumption Survey 1985," (November, 1988) and Monthly Energy Review, December, 1989 (March 1990) as reported by Price Waterhouse, "Background Material on Energy Excise Taxes," August 13, 1990.

43. Congress of the United States, Congressional Budget Office. *Federal Taxation of Tobacco, Alcoholic Beverages, and Motor Fuels* (Washington, D.C.: U.S. Government Printing Office, August 1990), and Greenstein, Robert and Frederick C. Hutchinson. "Offsetting the Effects of Regressive Tax Increases on Low and Moderate Income Households" (Washington, D.C.: Center on Budget and Policy Priorities, July 1990).

44. The CBO analysis covers the first two program elements, the second two are detailed in the CBPP publication.

45. Aaron, H.J., "The Value-Added Tax: Sorting Through the Practical and Political Problems," *The Brookings Review,* Summer 1988.

46. Conversation with Meg Powers, Community Action Foundation.

47. Burtrow has argued that the most appropriate compensation scheme for many environmental programs is to link compensation directly to the source or type of harm. The simplest interpretation of this principle would be to compensate job losses with job training programs or new employment opportunities. *See* Burtrow, D., "Compensating Losers when Cost-Effective Environmental Policies are Adopted," *Resources,* Resources for the Future, No. 104, Washington, D.C., 1991.

48. This estimate is in 1990 dollars and assumes a 10 percent real discount rate. Energy Information Administration, *Studies in Energy Taxes,* pages 32 and 35.

49. Dertouzos, Michael L., Richard K. Lester, and Robert M. Solow, *Made in America: Regaining the Productive Edge,* MIT Press, Cambridge, MA, 1989.

50. A recent report by the Office of Technology Assessment identifies several federal policy options that could help reduce the cost of capital to U.S. firms and thus improve their competitive positioning. Office of Technology Assessment, *Making Things Better—Competing in Manufacturing,* U.S. Congress, Washington, D.C., 1990.

51. Products manufactured from carbon-based fuels may be associated with other forms of pollution, but this is potentially true of all products and all economic activity. With or without a feedstock exemption, a carbon tax would not preclude the use of other pollution taxes. Trying to make a carbon tax reflect environmental concerns beyond climate change, however, could be problematic at best.

52. *See:* Hoeller, P. and M. Wallin. *Energy Prices, Taxes and Carbon Dioxide Emission,* Economics and Statistics Department Working Papers, No. 106 (Paris: Organization for Economic Co-Operation and Development 1991).

53. Communication From the Commission To the Council, *A Community Strategy To Limit Carbon Dioxide Emissions and To Improve Energy Efficiency,* Annex 7, Pg. 20. These figures are based on 1990 prices and exchange rates, are modulated according to a 50%/50% energy/carbon tax, and assume that the tax will be completely passed on to the energy user (first round effects).

54. The other two areas requiring unanimous approval are the free movement of persons and the rights and interests of employed persons.

World Resources Institute

1709 New York Avenue, N.W.
Washington, D.C. 20006, U.S.A.

The World Resources Institute (WRI) is a policy research center created in late 1982 to help governments, international organizations, and private business address a fundamental question: How can societies meet basic human needs and nurture economic growth without undermining the natural resources and environmental integrity on which life, economic vitality, and international security depend?

Two dominant concerns influence WRI's choice of projects and other activities:

The destructive effects of poor resource management on economic development and the alleviation of poverty in developing countries; and

The new generation of globally important environmental and resource problems that threaten the economic and environmental interests of the United States and other industrial countries and that have not been addressed with authority in their laws.

The Institute's current areas of policy research include tropical forests, biological diversity, sustainable agriculture, energy, climate change, atmospheric pollution, economic incentives for sustainable development, and resource and environmental information.

WRI's research is aimed at providing accurate information about global resources and population, identifying emerging issues, and developing politically and economically workable proposals.

In developing countries, WRI provides field services and technical program support for governments and non-governmental organizations trying to manage natural resources sustainably.

WRI's work is carried out by an interdisciplinary staff of scientists and experts augmented by a network of formal advisors, collaborators, and cooperating institutions in 50 countries.

WRI is funded by private foundations, United Nations and governmental agencies, corporations, and concerned individuals.